© Sweet Light Studio

Cyndi Dale is an internationally renowned author, speaker, and healer. She has written more than thirty books, including *Llewellyn's Complete Book of Chakras*; *Energy Healing for Trauma, Stress, and Chronic Illness*; *Kundalini*; and *The Complete Book of Chakra Healing*. Her year-long apprenticeship program through her company, Essential Energy, assists individuals in developing their natural intuitive and healing gifts. She also teaches in-depth classes via The Shift Network. Visit her at CyndiDale.com.

ROOT CHAKRA

YOUR FIRST ENERGY CENTER
SIMPLIFIED + APPLIED

EDITED BY
CYNDI DALE

Llewellyn Publications
WOODBURY, MINNESOTA

FIRST EDITION
First Printing, 2023

Book design by Rebecca Zins
Cover design by Cassie Willett
Illustrations on pages 16 and 109 by Llewellyn Art Department

Llewellyn is a registered trademark of Llewellyn Worldwide Ltd.

Library of Congress Cataloging-In-Publication Data

pending

ISBN 9780738772691

Llewellyn Publications
A Division of Llewellyn Worldwide Ltd.
2143 Wooddale Drive
Woodbury, MN 55125-2989
www.llewellyn.com
Printed in the United States of America

CONTENTS

PRACTICES

INTRODUCTION

What do you get when you mix glowing health, a zest for a career calling, material wealth, happy housing, sexual zip, a supersized sense of security, and all the energy you need to thrive physically?

You gain the benefits of a vigorous first chakra. I call the first chakra the "earth-star" chakra because it grounds and empowers at the same time. Called *muladhara* in Hindu tradition, the original source of most modern chakra knowledge, this is the subtle energy center that lies in your hip area, and it's the incredibly enriching subject of this book.

For seekers of a great life, it's vital to understand and interact with all of your chakras, and you'll be learning how to do that one chakra at a time in Llewellyn's Chakra Essentials, my eight-book series. The first seven of these books will each focus on a single chakra. Of course it makes sense to begin at the beginning; that's why you'll be treated to all things first chakra in this initial book in the series. Also known as your primal, root, and base chakra, this red-based energy ball is the starting point for creating a good life on every level, especially materially. (About that eighth book—more on that later!)

Your first chakra is literally the first step on a staircase that leads up from the base of your spine and toward enlightenment. Like all chakras, it is considered a "spinning wheel of light," as described in ancient Hindu scripture's beautiful Sanskrit language. However, the influence of chakra knowledge is worldwide, stretching way beyond the Indus Plain. That's because nearly every culture has interacted with an equivalent of the chakras. It's also because chakras are made of energy, which may be defined as "information that moves." There are two types of energy, and herein lies the crux of a chakra's power.

Physical energy describes the concrete stuff of our natural world and bodies. Ideally, it's important to comprehend how physical energy works. It comprises your bodily organs, the air you breathe, the food you eat, and anything else that is solid—but more than 99.999 percent of any object, including your body, is made up of subtle energy.[1]

Subtle energy is harder to measure than physical energy, but it decides what will appear in three-dimensional reality and what will not. Picture subtle energies as tiny little pin-

---

1 Ali Sundermier, "99.9999999% of Your Body Is Empty Space," September 23, 2016, https://www.sciencealert.com/99-9999999 -of-your-body-is-empty-space.

pricks and waves of light and sound. Together, they form the lattices or templates upon which physical elements organize. Do you know what coordinates the movement and management of your subtle energies? That's right: the "brains" of your subtle energy system—your chakras.

For perspective, it's helpful to understand that chakras are one of three structures that compose a greater subtle energy system. Your physical body's anatomy is made of three basic structures: your organs, channels, and fields. Your subtle body's anatomy is too; besides the chakras, your energy anatomy also includes channels and fields. I will share a few words about these now because they'll show up later in this book.

There are two types of subtle channels linked to the chakras: the meridians and the nadis. *Meridians* flow through the connective tissue and distribute subtle energy through the body. They are best known in Asian medical systems. The *nadis* also stream through the physical body but are mainly equivalent to your nerves. They will be highlighted in this book because the most important nadis interface with your chakras.

As well, every chakra creates its own field of energy. Altogether, these auric fields compose the greater auric field. Each emanation circles the body, interweaving among the others, to surround you in a protective field of light and sound. You'll learn a little about the first auric field in this book since it's produced by the first chakra.

Overall, there are seven in-body chakras and five found outside the body. Like the other six in-body chakras, your first chakra anchors in the spine. As every chakra does, no matter its location, your root chakra regulates specific physical, psychological, and spiritual functions. As with all the chakras, your first chakra is a land unto itself. To truly plumb its depths, it's imperative to understand it in its totality.

You might wonder why I work with a twelve-chakra system. I developed this model decades ago based on chakras I saw as a child, followed by research.

When I was young, I didn't know that the balls of light and sound I saw and heard emanating from and floating around people and animals were called chakras. Norwegian Lutherans like me didn't exactly use Sanskrit terms for such anomalies, but I knew they were important.

They changed hue and tone with my loved ones' moods. These fascinating orbs were so instructive that I often gauged my own actions by what was happening with their coloration. If my mom gave off a lot of muddy red energy, I stayed out of her way. It meant that she was mad and might take it out on me. If my dad came home from work shining with sunny yellow light, I knew he'd play with me.

If the yellow was muddy? I'd go to my room and do my own thing.

Eventually, I pursued further knowledge about these energy centers and related concepts through a decades-long odyssey. I worked with healers and shamans in Belize, Peru, Morocco, Venezuela, Russia, Costa Rica, the British Isles, and other places where indigenous cultures were keeping alive knowledge about energy, healing, intuition, spirits, and energetic anatomies. I studied spiritual and scientific tracts and worked with my own clients and students. I also discovered that chakra systems around the world had various numbers of chakras or other subtle energy bodies numbering anywhere between three and dozens. Along the way, I discovered that there was nothing universal about a seven-chakra system.

Why has the seven-chakra system become standard? It turns out that a particular spiritual author, Sir John Woodroffe, wrote a book in the early twentieth century[2] indicating that the Hindus prescribed to a seven-chakra system. Well, he actually didn't say that. He proposed a six-chakra system and added a spiritual one at the top of the head, and that was that. Westerners took to his model even though he actually said there are many chakra systems

---

2   *The Serpent Power* (Madras, India: Ganesh & Co.), reprinted 2003.

throughout India that testify to anywhere from three to dozens of chakras. And so it goes; we don't always question our experts, do we?

Since its inception, my twelve-chakra system has become a favored template around the world. I believe you'll love learning all about the five out-of-body chakras in my eighth book in this series, as it will greatly enhance your understanding of yourself and your place in the universe.

So, what's in this book, your first passport to adventure? In part 1 I'll present the foundational details of your first chakra in three chapters, drawing from ancient and modern knowledge. In the first chapter, I'll cover the fundamentals of your base chakra. This chapter will include the overarching purpose, location, various names, color, and sound of the chakra. Also relayed will be the associated elements, breaths, lotus petals, god and goddess, and so much more, including an initial description of the interconnection between the famous Shakti kundalini and her home, the first chakra. Kundalini is a special life energy that yogis have cultivated in East Indian and other cultures for thousands of years. By necessity, you must have at least a partial understanding of it to better your education about the first chakra.

In chapter 2 we'll look at the physicality of your first chakra. This exploration will include a deep dive into the organs and physical systems regulated by the first chakra as well as the material life issues that it manages.

We'll round the corner and complete our part 1 circuit in chapter 3 with an exploration of the psychological and spiritual functions of your base chakra. The ultimate goal is to gain a better sense of how your first chakra aids you in developing the sense of identity you need to materially thrive. We'll also cover intuitive attributes of this energy center and finalize our initial discussion of the kundalini.

In part 2 you'll be treated to the knowledge of additional energy experts who will serve as your go-to coaches for life improvement. I've mindfully selected each of these authors because they are among the best of the best in their fields, and their contributions add up to a chock-full book on the first chakra. You'll learn numerous methods for balancing and strengthening this chakra through yoga poses, spirit allies, shapes, colors, meditations, mantras, and so much more—even first-chakra-fueling recipes!

All in all, my goal is to present you with a book that you can resource over and over again. Who among us doesn't want to grasp our dreams as reflected in the stars and then plant them in the good earth? Open these pages and meet your first chakra and your earth-star, well-rooted self.

PART 1

ESTABLISHING THE FOUNDATION
OF YOUR FIRST CHAKRA KNOWLEDGE

• • • • • •

Breathe into your lower hip area. Focus first on your coccyx (tailbone), then notice the pulsing of electrical power that moves up and down your spine and throughout your body.

Reader, meet your root chakra: the subtle energy center that regulates all levels of your physical and material well-being.

This simultaneously earth-rich and star-flame chakra is your key to leading a fulfilling and secure life. It pulses with passion and purpose, and it can make sure your everyday life does too.

In this part of the book, you're going to learn all the fundamentals required to fully embrace and really enjoy your first chakra.

In the first chapter, I'll share information we've inherited from ancient Hindu culture, with a few modern twists thrown in. Then I'll hand out scuba equipment so we can deep-dive into the physical aspects of this rich wellspring of life energy. And in the third chapter, we'll delve into the psychological and spiritual functions of this primal and vital chakra. Ultimately you'll find yourself standing at the juncture of yesterday and today, ready to create your tomorrow.

1

FUNDAMENTALS

When it comes down to it, your first chakra's main job is to formulate rocket fuel for your body. Who doesn't need zip to zigzag, pizzazz to progress, and z's when it's siesta time?

Little wonder I call it the earth-star chakra; it provides the passion you need to take off while keeping your feet on solid ground. You'll learn all the basics about this chakra in this chapter.

First I'll provide insights about the most central purpose of this chakra by sharing a client case. (I'll give you a hint: your root chakra makes life energy.) I'll then present bite-size summations of the other first chakra essentials—information that has been assembled across time and rooted in the Hindu origins of chakra knowledge. Add up these puzzle pieces and you'll discover an amazing source of worldly power.

THE ESSENCE OF YOUR FIRST CHAKRA

I once worked with a woman who was completely exhausted. She could barely drag herself out of bed in the morning. Once on her feet, she suffered through the day, continually fatigued. Everyday tasks were gargantuan endeavors. She felt lucky if she could check a few priorities off her to-do list each day—the rest were added to her next day's undertakings.

Can you imagine how long her list was after a few months of this?

When someone is that weary, it's necessary to look for causes on every level, including medical causes. From an energy point of view, however, I knew we were looking at first chakra challenges because the first chakra is all about our physical existence. When something is wrong with the body—or any concrete life necessity—the subtle energetics of that problem involve the first chakra.

I wasn't surprised when her physician discovered an adrenal disease. As you'll learn in the next chapter, the endocrine gland linked to the first chakra is the adrenals. Once my client received treatment for that disorder, she perked up dramatically.

For our current purposes, this story illuminates your first chakra's essential nature. It produces material energy for your body. If this chakra is off, at some level you'll experience a physical deficit. The symptoms might include a bodily disorder like the one my client exhibited.

It's just as likely that you could be struck by a different basic life issue, such as one (or many) involving finances, shelter, nourishment, and more. Because the psyche is so integrated with the body, you might also face any number of emotional or mental challenges and even spiritual loss. Throughout the rest of part 1, you'll learn about a variety of physical and psychological problems that a weak first chakra might cause as well as the gains you will receive when you actively support this chakra, which invites a rooted, well-grounded life. The takeaway, for now, is this: everything most of us desire in order to thrive is dependent on having a healthy first chakra.

Overarching Purpose

Your first chakra rules your physical energy and drives self-preservation. When it's healthy, it assures safety, survival, and material thriving.

IT'S ALL IN THE NAME: TERMS FOR THE FIRST CHAKRA

One of the ways to obtain a clear understanding about an important topic is to delve into the meanings of the names assigned to it. I'm going to examine a few of the names for the first chakra to help us do exactly this.

The most traditional designations for all the chakras are derived from the Hindu religion, which originally employed the symbolic language of Sanskrit to depict important terms.

The Sanskrit name for the first chakra is *muladhara*. The word combines *mul*, or base, with *adhara*, or support. This nomenclature wonderfully describes the first chakra's main goal: to root and sustain us in daily life.

There are many other names referencing the first chakra in ancient Hindu literature. Labels used in the later Upanishads, one of the primary sources of the Hindu teachings, include *Brahma*, the name of the universal god, and *mulakanda*, which references a part of a root. Tantric texts often include the word *padma* in relation to the first chakra, which is the designation for the lotus, one of the most common symbols of all chakras. All names for the first chakra recognize its primal nature as well as your own.

LOCATION OF THE FIRST CHAKRA

One of the reasons this chakra is called the root chakra is that it governs the entire lower hip area, front and back sides. Quite literally, this area roots your spine. It is also described as being anchored at the base of the spine and in the groin. Given this latter location, it is often considered the major sexual chakra.

Like all seven in-body chakras, your first chakra is linked to an area of the spine: specifically, the sacrococcygeal nerve plexus. That area includes your coccyx and three of the vertebrae atop it.

Some experts believe muladhara lies between the anus and scrotum in men and near the back of the cervix in women. Others believe it can be found just below the *kanda*, an energetic organ located between the anus and the root of the reproductive organ. I'll explain the kanda in the next chapter.

If you want an even more specific set of directions, you can open the ancient Hindu tract called the *Sat-Cakra Nirupana* and follow its instructions, which say that the first chakra is two finger-widths above the anus, two finger-widths below the genitals, and four fingers wide.[3]

You can see your first chakra on figure 1, the twelve-chakra system. Note that the twelfth chakra is an energetic field that surrounds the body.

---

3   Purnananda-Svami, "Sat Chakra Nirupana," https://www
.bhagavadgitausa.com/sat_chakra_Nirupana.pdf.

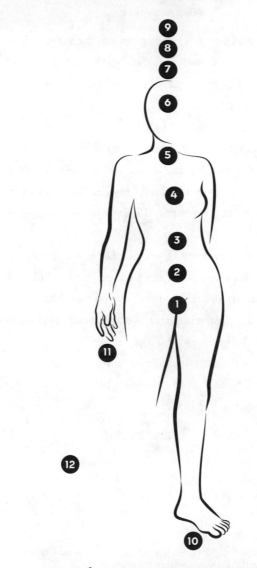

FIGURE 1: THE TWELVE-CHAKRA SYSTEM

COLOR OF THE FIRST CHAKRA

Every chakra manages a different set of frequencies, or bands of energy. These can be described by color and sound. I'll talk about the first chakra's sound in the next section.

Regarding color, the first chakra processes all the subtle energies in the red spectrum. You'll enjoy learning various ways to employ colors to clear and clean your first chakra in chapter 12.

Red is the perfect depiction of the first chakra. It is a primal pigment, the hue of blood. As such, it is energizing, passionate, and stimulating. It oxygenates—physically, emotionally, and spiritually—and assures a healthy and hale lifestyle. It is the color of life.

Red also represents the Hindu goddess Shakti. You'll learn a lot about Shakti throughout part 1 because her power is intertwined with the first chakra's functions and authority. Shakti, also known as Parvati, Durga, and Kali, is one of the most important goddesses of the Hindu pantheon. When she is called Shakti Dakini, she is appearing as the ruler of the first chakra. Often this is also the term assigned her as the consort of Lord Shiva, a supreme god we will also be interacting with in part 1.

Shakti exemplifies the primordial cosmic energy that moves through the universe. Her many personalities add up to the preeminent Earth Mother, the active dynamic that creates, maintains, and destroys the universe. Without Shakti there would be no aliveness, no creation, no transformation.

Within the body Shakti is associated with the activation of the kundalini, a primal life force that rises from the first chakra to stimulate the healing of our issues and activate enlightenment. The force of kundalini is also called the red or serpent kundalini.

There is a secondary color associated with the first chakra: black. Black is considered a mystical color. Many practitioners across time have recommended healing stones for the first chakra that are black, brown, silver, or another earthen color. Hence, black can be seen to depict the grounding nature of the first chakra. No matter what, the first chakra's hues reinforce its attributes as the provider of stability, support, and roots into the earth.

SOUND OF THE FIRST CHAKRA

In modern times, the root chakra has become related to the C note on the musical scale. Throughout Hindu history, the sound associated with the first chakra has always been *Lam*, pronounced "lum." Lam is often associated with the Hindu god Indra, the king of the gods and defender of humankind against evil. It is also the tone of spiritual awakening.

There are many terms used to label the tone held within each chakra. These tones are called bijas (seed sounds) as well as bija mantras, or master sounds. A mantra is a sound that encourages a meditative state.

Sound Carrier

A special being is considered the carrier of the first chakra sound: the *airavata*, or elephant with seven trunks.

In Indian mythology, the elephant represents abundance and wisdom and embodies Brahma, the creator. It brings wealth to the owner, and the elephant's brain personifies a brilliant pearl of unbelievable value. This is the wisdom that allows us to reach higher consciousness.

The seven trunks of the elephant also symbolize the seven basic materials of the body, as well as the seven minerals and precious gems in the earth. Finally, the elephant reflects seven levels of consciousness: unconsciousness, subconsciousness, dream consciousness, waking consciousness, astral consciousness, supreme consciousness, and cosmic consciousness.

LOTUS PETALS AND APPEARANCE

Lotus petals are a well-known depiction of the in-body chakras. Every chakra exhibits a specific number and color of petals.

At one level, the petals depict the swirling motion of a chakra as it brings in and releases the subtle energies related to its band of frequencies. Chakras are also affected by the movements of the physical organs, fluids, and electromagnetic field (EMF) activity in their localized areas. If you were to freeze-frame the spiraling energies of a chakra, you would perceive a vortex with several outstretching arms of EMF. Those arms would appear like lotus flower petals.

Lotuses are highly valued in Indian society as a symbol of a spiritual life. They grow in muddy water, yet the flowers always stand clear of the water. The water is the *maya*, or illusion of life, and the blossoms are our true selves.

The first chakra's lotus is called *mula kamala*. It features four petals, each of which denote the four points of the compass as well the psychic functions of the mind, intellect, consciousness, and ego. The petals also epitomize the four developmental stages of planetary life: vegetation (such as single-cell organisms); egg-laying animals (including fish, reptiles, and birds); mammals; and humans.

The petals are red, and each is imprinted with a letter of gold. These letters are va, scha, sha, and sa. Each represents a vibration of one of four nadis, which are the channels of energy that interconnect the chakras and mirror the nerves in the body.

FIRST CHAKRA SYMBOLS:
THE YANTRAS

A yantra is a geometric diagram. Yantras were used over 13,000 years ago in Indian religions to aid in meditation. Different yantras also embody various gods and goddesses, and when they are focused on, they invite power and healing from a deity. They can also exemplify certain tasks or vows.

The yantra, or representative symbol, for the first chakra is a yellow square surrounded by four red petals and eight spears. The latter represent the eight directions.

The square contains a downward-pointing triangle; inside is the bija, or seed symbol. Above or near this seed symbol are images of the child Brahma, who is colored red and has four faces and arms. In three hands he carries a staff, a gourd, and a mala (similar to a rosary); with his empty hand, he makes a gesture to dispel fear. With him is Shakti Dakini—the Shakti who is the *dakini*, or ruler, of the first chakra. She is red and has four arms that hold a spear, a skull staff, a sword, and a drinking cup. A white elephant is located under the lower point of the triangle. Also within the yantra is a representation of kundalini, coiled three and a half times around the Shiva lingam. Shiva is a male god who is considered the mate of Shakti. A lingam is a symbol or mark. So, the Shiva lingam is the mark of Shiva.

The inverted triangle is called the trikona. Also called kama, it represents the dormant kundalini, although it is considered fiery and filled with the energy of desire. It denotes the yoni, or female energy, and points downward to show that we are in the initial stages of our spiritual development. The sides of the triangle spread upward and outward to reflect the direction of a developing consciousness.

The lingam inside symbolizes male energy and is an important Hindu symbol. Black, it represents the color of matter. The Shiva lingam references creativity and consciousness; in fact, the three rotations of the serpent relate to three levels of consciousness: unconscious, subconscious, and conscious. The half-turn refers to the awakened superconsciousness. The serpent head points downward to indicate that we can evolve—or devolve. The snake is also known as kala, or the collective aspects of time: past, present, and future. Together, the yoni and lingam represent the opposites of the physical world. (See the granthi section for further information about the lingam.)

GROSS ELEMENT

In Hinduism, all matter is made up of four basic elements: earth, water, fire, and wind/air. Many systems also endorse a fifth element: space. The first chakra's element is earth.

The earth (*prithvi*) element contains the qualities of solidness and attractive forces. The latter means that the earth element can magnetize and compact matter. The presence of this element is one of the reasons the first chakra is called the base or root chakra, which links us to the earth.

At this point, you probably perceive why I personally call the first chakra the "earth-star" chakra. In doing so, I'm emphasizing the power of a star and its fire, particularly the red fire. The earth element adds sturdiness. Interestingly, planet Earth itself is ablaze with the type of energy that activates within the first chakra. Some esoterics believe that the center of the earth is equivalent to a dwarf star.

A chakra isn't just one thing; it is many things. Your first chakra provides you with the poetry of your dreams and the activity of doing. It gives both life and a reason for it. Who doesn't want to root into some lovely and powerful combination of earth and star?

Color of the Gross Element

In Hinduism, the earth element is considered yellow. Yellow symbolizes spring, knowledge, and stability. Imagine yourself in the sun and you'll feel the brightness and hopefulness of this element. It also illuminates the potentiality of new beginnings.

PREDOMINANT SENSE
AND SENSORY ORGAN

Each of the main seven chakras is associated with a sense and a sensory organ. This is exciting because we so often think of chakras as ethereal. The truth is that these subtle organs also manage our physical selves. Through the first chakra, you draw upon the sense of smell through the organ of the nose.

The sense of smell and the nose organ are intricately associated with the psychological development of the newborn self, which is quite fitting for the first chakra. You'll also learn in the next two chapters that this chakra is initiated in utero through six months of age. It is your most primal chakra, given that smell is the most archaic or primitive of all five senses. Without knowing it, we depend on smell to make all sorts of decisions, from deciding whether a person is attractive to assessing the safety of a room.

You can boost the health of your first chakra through your sense of smell by employing scents that you personally associate with being healthy and vital. One way to do this is to light candles or use aromatherapy that you associate with happy memories. When I was growing up, we made gingerbread cookies and decorated them every Christmas. When I light a gingerbread and clove candle in the house, I feel warm, stable, and happy. Following is a practice you can use to draw upon the sense and sense organ of your first chakra.

SPECIAL MULADHARA RITUAL: "KNOWING YOUR NOSE"

Want to access your first chakra? One way is to perform the nasikagra drishti. This is a ritual that involves gazing at the tip of your nose until you develop the ability, over time, to smell psychic fragrances. This practice is also called the agochari mudra, the gesture of invisibility. A mudra is a special gesture that enables a higher outcome.

Here is how to perform this practice:

» Sit comfortably and gaze ahead, breathing normally. Relax your shoulders and place your palms on your knees.

» Slowly move your eyes so you are staring at the tip of your nose. Keep your gaze here for only a few seconds, holding your breath while doing so. If you feel pain, return your gaze to normal.

» Repeat this process in one sitting for as long as you can, and then return to it later, making sure not to strain your eyes.

» Practice for several months and see if you can develop a higher state of consciousness, including the sense of smell when you are thinking about a certain event, person, or situation. For instance, when preparing by sitting comfortably and gazing about normally, deliberately take a few deep breaths, then focus on a person or situation. Is there a smell that arises? While staring at the tip of your nose, allow your inner self to relate to that smell and how you feel about it. Every time you reiterate that step, again think of your subject and see if you can change the aroma you associate with it—and consequently your memories, emotions, or opinions.

ACTION ORGAN

Every in-body chakra is connected to an action organ. This is the part of the body that brings physical energy to that chakra and that the chakra supplies with vitality in turn. The action organ of the first chakra is your feet. You can be assured that your first chakra pumps lots of life energy upward into your body and downward into your legs by making sure you walk often.

VITAL BREATH

In Hinduism the most vital life force is called prana. The other label for prana is "vital principle." Prana permeates all reality and is considered a subtle energy. The dense or obvious manifestation of prana is the breath.

There are five different types of vital prana. The first chakra is associated with one of these vital breaths: apana. Apana is linked with elimination and governs the exhalation of the breath, release of digestive wastes, and all aspects of menstruation.

ATTRIBUTE

An attribute is a quality. The elephant, the carrier of the first chakra sound, is known for being patient. That is the main quality of the first chakra. It is what we obtain when we cultivate our root chakra. The opposite, which is greed, can also take hold if we fail to learn patience.

RULING GODDESS(ES)

A goddess is associated with each of the main chakras from the Hindu point of view. The most frequently mentioned of these for the first chakra is Shakti Dakini, previously noted in the symbols/yantra section. As the dakini, Shakti is the gatekeeper of physical reality.

RULING GOD(S)

This chakra is usually attributed to Brahma, the creator of physical reality, also described in the yantra section. However, the goal of the kundalini, the essential energy associated with Shakti in the body, is to merge with Shiva in the crown, or seventh, chakra. We'll discuss this kundalini process throughout the next two chapters.

RULING PLANET

The planet ruling your first chakra is Saturn, an earthy force that teaches us about our limits. That planet is also associated with hard work. Life is very much about providing lessons that lead to the development of patience and maturity.

GRANTHI (KNOT)

Granthi are the "locks" the kundalini must pass through in order to ascend. Think of a lock as a knot in a rope, a sort of riddle we must unwind before we can continue with the greater things of life. There are three granthi, or locks, in the subtle anatomy. The first of these is associated with the first chakra.

The first chakra lock is called the Brahma granthi, or Knot of Brahma. We unravel it to release the illusion of the earth as a prison. To release this knot, we must stop resisting change. Once we've done this, the knot unbinds and the kundalini can rise. This process includes accessing the power of the Shiva lingam, also called the *swayambhu linga*. *Swayambhu* means self-reproduced. This linga assists us in embodying our true selves.

RELATED AURIC FIELD

The related auric field for the first chakra is the first auric layer, located just outside the skin. I perceive it interpenetrating the skin and then extending to about an inch and a half around the entire body.

This field is controlled by the programs found inside the first chakra. These programs come from any number of sources, including the experiences and beliefs of our ancestors, influences within our family of origin, childhood and adult events, external society, and other influences. Based on these programs, which operate like computer codes, the first auric field filters the subtle energies that match the first chakra. If you want to alter the types of situations, people, or material goods you are attracting or deflecting, you must change the programs in the first chakra. Many of the practices provided in part 2 will help you do this.

BENEATH YOUR FIRST CHAKRA

There are additional chakras and realms of existence that lie below and are associated with your first chakra. Of note are seven minor chakras below the first chakra. These descend downward along the leg. They are called *talas*, and they look like shadowy material spheres. While the first chakra is largely related to the material plane, manifesting, and sexuality, the lower chakras are linked to experiences of a lower nature, or various types of evil.

The seven lower chakras/talas are each connected to a cosmic realm or plane. These planes are called *lokas*. They look like luminous spheres. In many chakra systems, there are seven lower lokas and seven higher lokas in total.

A long time ago, these spheres described various levels of existence. Now they are comparable to aspects of consciousness, one leading to another. In relation to the root chakra, we pay attention to the lower seven lokas, each of which relates to a lower tala that lies underneath the first chakra.

These lower lokas are often compared to a ring of hell, one of the layers in the underworld that invites us to meet a temptation and come out stronger. In Hinduism, the state of hell is called *naraka*.

The lower lokas are as follows:

CHAKRA	LOCATION	GOVERNS
ATALA	HIPS	FEAR AND LUST
VITALA	THIGHS	ANGER AND RESENTMENT
SUTALA	KNEES	JEALOUSY
TALATALA	CALVES	PROLONGED CONFUSION AND WILLFULNESS
RASATALA	ANKLES	SELFISHNESS AND PURE ANIMAL NATURE
MAHATALA	FEET	THE DARK REALM, THE SPACE WITHOUT CONSCIENCE; INNER BLINDNESS
PATALA	SOLES OF FEET	MALICE, MURDER, TORTURE, AND HATRED; HELL

SUMMARY

As you've learned, your muladhara—or your first, base, or root chakra—is the base of your existence. Within it the kundalini lies coiled, awaiting her climb. In the meantime—and across all time—this core chakra busily hums along, regulating safety, security, and your fundamental life and death functions.

Colored red and toned with *Lam,* carried by the seven-trunked elephant, your root chakra is anchored in the coccygeal vertebrae. Physically, it relates to the sense of smell and the nose and employs the active organ of the feet. Its symbols are a yellow square with four red petals and eight spears, and it reflects the earth element, which is yellow. It holds the vital breath of apana and the attribute of patience. (Don't we all need more of that?)

Herein you connect with the Shakti and Brahma and can implement the rays of Saturn. Once you've worked through the Knot of Brahma, you're well on your way to forging a life of safety and joy, expressing your needs through your first auric field and working through the lokas, or cosmic planes of hell and temptation. All in all, your first chakra provides the essential energy you need for a successful material life, which is why it's sometimes helpful to think of it as an earth-star chakra, helping us merge the reality of the physical existence with the dreams of our soul.

Now that you've considered the ancient and modern fundamentals of your first chakra, let's delve into the physicality of this brightly lit chakra.

2

THE PHYSICAL SIDE

Though most of reality consists of subtle energy, the first chakra's most vital work is to help us provide for ourselves and others materially. To do this, it rules the geography of the lower hips and the adrenals, its associated endocrine gland. As you'll learn in this chapter, it also has a unique secondary home. This is a very concrete area of the spine that the Hindus call the *kanda*. Wait until you find out how critical it is to your health and well-being!

Through this chapter's focus on the physical functions of your muladhara, you'll also learn about the most critical disease processes that can affect it, as well as the more earthly—think physical—role of the kundalini.

OVERVIEW OF THE
FIRST CHAKRA'S PHYSICAL REACH

Your root chakra is a chakra of matter. That means it is essential to you, and it also means that it assists in regulating all the physical matter that creates a well-adjusted, successful life.

It begins regulating your life energy at conception, assuring that your life force is shared among all cells throughout your embryonic development. The instinct for survival is programmed from the get-go, and your first chakra makes sure that every molecule and organ operates in concert to give life and defer death. Because of this, this base chakra is intricately involved in the fight, flight, freeze, and fawn reactions to stress. Your most primal and physical responses to situations that are opportunistic or endangering are tasked to this chakra.

The first chakra is energetically key to the rising of the kundalini, a process we briefly talked about in the previous chapter. From a biological point of view, the rise of kundalini is not only a spiritual progression but also a biochemical and electrical one.

Every cell in the body pulses with electricity, the most fundamental of life energies. Electricity produces more electricity, magnetism, and electromagnetism. All these measurable forms of light are created through the shifting of electrons in our atoms and the movements of subatomic particles, as well as the ionization of minerals found in the body such as sodium, magnesium, potassium, and calcium.

One of the reasons the ancients emphasized the importance of an active kundalini is that at baseline, the rising of kundalini is the rising of electricity in the spine. Plain and simple, when the electrical flow of energies in your body is high and smooth, you will be healthy. You will also produce the electromagnetic fields around your body (known collectively as the biofield) that will keep you safe and secure. If the electrical flow is low and disheveled, your life will be the same.

As I've already shared, this chakra's primary development starts in the womb—at conception—and is accentuated during the six months after birth. I'll speak about the psychological effects of this developmental stage in the next chapter, but right now I want to emphasize the link between this chakra's physical rulership and your fundamental life needs.

If your primal needs were met in these early stages of life, this chakra will develop a healthy set of life energy programs. Did your mom eat healthy food when she was pregnant with you? Were the foundational material needs of your family met during the in utero period and first months of life? Were you able to employ your sense of smell and the sensory organ of your nose to "root around" and be fed?

First chakra—and basic life—necessities include shelter, clean air, food, water, and money for provisions. Also included are affection, loving touch, and emotionally available guardians. If any one of these was deficient, it will be hard to overcome the resulting sense of lack and limitation, as well as any of the array of physical disorders you might be susceptible to.

In other words, our most elementary experiences of safety and security will program this chakra. If our experiences were positive overall, we'll be able to provide for ourselves financially, relationally, and environmentally. We'll choose to eat nourishing food, select supportive sexual partners or mates, and be able to make and retain a living. If our experiences were restricted or abusive, our material success and physical health will be challenged.

AREAS OF THE BODY MANAGED

The first chakra manages a full palette of bodily parts. In general, look to those located in the lower hip area. The physical organs' functions are also included in the first chakra's purview.

The bodily areas under the first chakra's umbrella include your muscles, hip joints, the coccygeal vertebra, the general immune system, the bladder, the rectum, the lower extremities (hips and related bones and muscles), the elimination system, the large intestine, the adrenals, and parts of the genitals, such as the vagina. It also shares responsibility with other chakras for the prostate and kidneys.

ASSOCIATED GLAND: THE ADRENALS

The root chakra is linked with the adrenal glands, two small organs that lie atop the kidneys. Understanding the physiology and functioning of the adrenals is an invitation to glimpsing the vital nature of your first chakra.

The adrenals are often called our "stress glands" because they emit hormones that respond instantaneously to stress. The adrenals are really two glands in one, with each section influential in its own way. The adrenal cortex secretes steroidal hormones such as cortisol, hydrocortisone, aldosterone, and DHEA, as well as small amounts of testosterone, estrogen, and progesterone, in both men and women. These regulate our long-term response to stress through such activities as monitoring blood sugar levels and balancing fluids.

The adrenal medulla emits adrenaline, the hormone that helps us respond to immediate stress. A burst of adrenaline increases our heart rate, muscle tension, and bodily sweat. This instantaneous response to stress isn't harmful; it helps us respond quickly to change or danger. In fact, having too few adrenal hormones isn't helpful; people with chronic fatigue syndrome appear to have underactive adrenal glands. Too much stimulation over time, however, causes the adrenals to malfunction.

After going into hyperdrive following a kick-start from the adrenals, we often experience the opposite: incredible fatigue during the day. Then, ironically, we shift back into high gear at night and are unable to sleep. Signs of adrenal dysfunction include anxiety, insomnia, frequent illnesses, low blood pressure (which eventually can turn into high blood pressure), mental chatter, fluctuating blood sugar, exhaustion following exercise, and emotionalism leading to depression.

In our busy society, we are constantly exposed to adrenal stressors. These range from excessive noise, challenges on the job or in finding suitable work, and an overburdened schedule of experiencing chronic anger, powerlessness, worry, fear, and guilt. We can stress ourselves out by skipping meals, eating too much sugar or junk food, and using addictive substances. We are also affected by trauma, unrelenting pain, long-term illness (our own or someone else's), allergies, or toxic exposure. Emotional, physical, mental, or spiritual threats to our basic security will also affect our adrenals—and therefore our first chakra.

As an energy healer, I have found that almost every client needs to address first chakra or adrenal-based issues.

One of the reasons I like working on adrenal challenges from a chakra standpoint is that I'm afforded a full range of healing options. Resolving imbalances in the first chakra helps my clients psychologically, physically, and spiritually. This is the purpose of chakra medicine.

RELATED PHYSICAL STRESSORS, PROBLEMS, AND ILLNESSES

Any life-or-death illness or stressor is associated with the first chakra. Chronic or terminal illnesses, the effects of long-term stress, and overwhelming acute or chronic pain always involve an imbalanced first chakra at some level. If you commonly find yourself fatigued, exhausted, or unable to perform such necessary life duties as getting to work, cooking your meals, or paying your bills, you're probably looking at some sort of first chakra disorder.

Likewise, if you're struggling with financial woes, sexual confusion or problems, family systems complications, life-threatening addictions or abuse experiences, or any other acute material struggles, the first chakra is involved.

The truth is that any critical survival challenge or life-threatening event can inhibit the first chakra's function. These can include hardships experienced by your ancestors, which are genetically transferred into your body during conception; negative in utero experiences; the failure of your

parents to meet your needs; material lack; exposure to addictions, abuse, and other trauma; and so much more. Basically, anything that threatened you or your family's survival
can injure your first chakra.

Illnesses associated with the first chakra include obe-
sity and other eating disorders; hemorrhoids; constipation;
sciatica; fibromyalgia; chronic fatigue; leg, knee, and foot
problems, including varicose veins; arthritis; skin problems;
disorders of the bones and teeth; disorders of the bowels, anus, or large intestine; problems with the base of the
spine; life-challenging addictions such as heavy drug use
and alcoholism; sexual dysfunctions; reproductive issues;
blood deficiencies, and life-threatening issues of any sort,
such as various cancers and autoimmune disorders.

THE SPECIAL ASSOCIATION WITH YOUR
NERVOUS SYSTEM: THE NADIS

Physically, the first chakra is completely intertwined with
the nervous system. I can best explain this connection with
a fuller description of the kundalini and its link with the
nadis than I provided in the last chapter.

When represented symbolically, kundalini is often por-
trayed as a serpent lying coiled at the base of our first
chakra. As I've shared, this serpent kundalini is red in color
and considered feminine. Wrapped around our coccyx, this

life energy is dormant until summoned, at which point she awakens and begins undulating upward.

She might be stirred for any number of reasons. Many people cultivate her awakening through rituals like meditation, exercise, yoga, mindful breathing, and more. Other times kundalini is activated by an acute or chronic stress, from rape to the loss of a job. Sometimes attending therapy can awaken it; when our issues stir and we devote ourselves to resolving them, those efforts might rouse the kundalini.

The path of this life energy is winding as it flows through the nadis, the energy channels that deliver subtle energy to the chakras. As the kundalini travels these pathways, it activates each of the seven in-body chakras. The goal of this potent feminine force is to reach the seventh chakra, which is located at the crown of the head and reflects a male energy. The merging of the feminine kundalini and her male consort atop the head enables full access to Spirit and invites enlightenment, called *samadhi* in Sanskrit. This unification of feminine and masculine forges a marriage between our own feminine and masculine selves as well as our human and divine qualities.

The nadis are partially comparable to the meridians of Asian medical systems. There are striking differences, however. Fourteen main meridians or channels deliver chi throughout the body. Chi is the term for life energy used in traditional Chinese medicine. Depending on the source text, Hindu scripture counts anywhere from 1,000 to 3,500 nadis. If you ask members of the Tibetan and Ayurvedic traditions, the latter being an East Indian healing modality and philosophy, you'll be told such numbers are far too low and that there are 72,000 nadis.

Some researchers believe that meridians interact with the duct system, the bodily tubes that carry glandular secretions, and nadis are associated with the physical nervous system. Under this scenario, the meridians and nadis fulfill different jobs. I too believe that the nadis are primarily associated with the nervous system—which, by the way, is an electrical conductor.

Whatever the similarities and differences, three main nadis are especially vital to the rising kundalini, and all of them are linked to the first chakra through the kanda, the core neurological structure associated with the root chakra and described in the next section.

The sushumna is the central energy channel that flows up the center of the spine through the chakras and serves as the main road for the rising kundalini. Its biochemical and electrical flow could be seen as emanating directly from the coccyx, the spinal home of the first chakra. Through the kanda, kundalini also splits itself in two and flows through two additional conduits, the ida and pingala.

The ida, which originates in the kanda and ends at the left nostril, is considered a feminine channel, and its energy is receptive, loving, and intuitive. The pingala starts at the kanda and ends at the right nostril. It is masculine in nature: demonstrative, dominating, and active. These crisscrossing energies ensure a blend of our own feminine and masculine qualities and activate the same within our chakras, which have similar attributes.

At one level, the ida can be linked to your parasympathetic nervous system, which gives relaxing messages to the body. The pingala is more closely associated with the sympathetic nervous system, which tells your body to shift into high gear. These two nervous system processes are part of the autonomic nervous system, which regulates your automated reactions to stress. They are also integral parts of the polyvagal nervous system.

These days, the understanding of health, stress, and emotions is equivalent to comprehending your polyvagal system. The polyvagal theory is that the two trunks of your autonomic nervous system (the relaxing parasympathetic, also split into two parts, and the frenzied sympathetic) interact with your enteric nervous system (your gut-based microbiome and neurotransmitters) and your vagus nerve (a long cranial nerve that runs downward through the body) to determine your social behavior and stress reactions. In the end, we're talking about the complexities of your nervous system that at some primal level are largely programmed by the types of issues that affect your first chakra.

THE KANDA:
THE NADI CHAKRA

The kanda chakra, also called the kundalini or nadi chakra, is an energy body that is linked to (and part of) the first chakra. It is found at the junction between the sushumna nadi and the top of the muladhara and is seen as a white egg shape covered with membranes. It serves as a "home sac" for the nadis. From this base, the nadis emerge and weave a network through and even beyond the body.

The four petals of muladhara cover each of the four sides of the kanda, and at their junction we find the Brahma granthi, discussed in the previous chapter.

In the physical body, the end of the spinal cord tapers off into a fine silken thread, including a strand of non-neural fibrous tissue called the filum terminale, which lends support to the spinal cord. This strand of delicate tissue passes downward from the conus medullaris, the tapered lower end of the spinal cord, and is made of two parts. The upper part is about 6 inches long as it reaches the lower border of the second sacral vertebra, and the lower part eventually attaches to the back side of the first segment of the coccyx.

The first chakra is often considered to be located at the base of the filum terminale.

Also emanating from the conus medullaris is the cauda equina, a bundle of spinal nerves and nerve roots that spread throughout the legs and hip area, including into the perineum and the bladder. This bundle is equated with the kanda. Because of its appearance, the cauda equina is named after a horse's tail.

This association is quite fitting, as many esoteric scholars believe that the root chakra is linked to the hips, perineum, and bladder, and that its effects extend downward like a root through the feet, connecting with the earth. As you learned in the previous chapter, there are several secondary chakras in the hips, legs, and feet, and in the description of the cauda equina, we find the scientific explanation for the existence of these chakras.

In working with the kanda chakra on clients, I have found that it energetically embodies the physical power-house that is this region of the body. I often stimulate this area of the body, either intuitively or by working with this energy field with my hands, for clients who are low in energy, dealing with life-and-death issues, or struggling with finances or any other bodily or "real life" concerns. At one point I worked on a woman with critical health issues, including several forms of heart disease and cancer. She felt a bolt of energy, and over the next few weeks she found that she could better cope with her various medical treatments. After six months her issues were seemingly cleared, save the need to continue with several prescription medications.

SUMMARY

Ancient and modern approaches to the first chakra meet as do crossroads. The first chakra has been known as the source of life energy for centuries. Once stirred, the kundalini rising out of the first chakra's kanda through the nadis has been seen to deliver bold powers throughout the system. As we've discussed, life energy—and specifically the kundalini—is comparable to the electricity that flows through our bodies, without which we would have no life.

Charged with programming the codes that regulate our electrical selves from conception, the first chakra is intimately involved in all aspects of our materiality, from physical health to material wealth. As such, the base chakra manages many of the organic functions related to the hip area of the body and is greatly affected by events occurring between conception and six months of age.

Many disease processes can be traced back to how our first chakra reacted to outside trauma and dysfunction, including our modern specialty: adrenal challenges. Who among us isn't at least somewhat exhausted by contemporary life, with our polyvagal system ready for change?

The broad understanding of the physical nature of your earth-star chakra will now make the information covered in the next chapter even more intriguing. Reader, meet the psyche and soul of the first chakra.

3

OF THE PSYCHE AND THE SOUL

For most of our ancestors, the words they used for *psyche* also meant "soul." So *psychology* is actually the "knowledge or study of the soul." Nowhere is this idea truer than when we become educated about the chakras.

In this chapter, you'll dig into the various psychological and spiritual facets of the root or earth-star chakra. As you'll discover, your first chakra has powerful effects on your emotional well-being, storing many of your hard-core feelings and beliefs, both positive and negative. Its relationship with the Shakti kundalini—which is the red or serpent kundalini that almost every yogic system discusses and cultivates—adds zest to its impact. Of special interest is the intuitive faculty linked to your first chakra, as it lends you insights into your everyday and higher decision making.

OVERARCHING PSYCHOLOGICAL IMPACT

The home of the sleeping kundalini, the Shakti power of transformation and change, your first chakra is responsible for issues related to your safety, security, survival, and basic needs. Because it is linked with the ida, pingala, and sushumna—the three energy channels that ascend the spine—the concepts stored within its memory banks affect your psychological well-being on the most fundamental of levels, often determining how you respond to stress.

When you're very young, this complex center takes on your family-of-origin beliefs, adding them to the karma your soul already carries. Karma constitutes the issues your soul must work through in order to embrace and give love. Many of the current life questions that all beings have about their place in the universe are transferred in from previous lives. The cycle of returning for one lifetime after another to gain spiritual maturity is called reincarnation. Your earth-star chakra also relays the dharma already achieved in previous existences. Dharma signifies the wisdom you've already gained, over multiple lifetimes, about the truth and power of love.

As the root chakra, this energy center is your primary anchor into your ancestry, family system, daily life, and foundational identity. Because of this chakra, you know that you exist. You acquire skills to assist you in getting beyond mere existence in order to become a fully realized person. And then the kundalini goes *kaboom*, and all aspects of you conjoin to invite even more transformation.

As I explore your muladhara from various psychological and spiritual angles, keep in mind that in the end it represents a singular irony. It is the seat of your kundalini, the fire energy often associated with sex. As such, it is at the core of your human drives and desires, yet it also reflects a quality of innocence, the pure and childlike joy that imparts honor, dignity, and a reliance on the Divine, no matter how very mundane your life experiences may be. This chakra blesses us all with the love of the Divine Mother, who is constantly available to help us overcome all challenges so we can transform them gracefully.

CHAKRA ACTIVATION

As I said in the previous chapter, this chakra activates from in utero to six months of age. It is lit up when the sperm and egg unite and life energy merges the fertilized egg with your own spirit, or eternal essence, and your soul, the vehicle for experience. Your first concern is to survive; the second is to be birthed.

If you are greeted with warmth, love, and nourishment, your first chakra will hold beliefs such as "Life is safe" and "It is good to be myself." If the opposite occurs, your foundational beliefs will be destructive. Examples include "The world is dangerous" and "Life is a struggle."

After birth, the first chakra interacts with primal considerations, realizing that life will or will not guarantee the provision of your basic needs, such as food, water, shelter, comfort, and calm sleep. While the body is developing at an incredible speed during the first chakra months, the psychological ideas being formed are contingent on the meeting of these needs.

PSYCHOLOGICAL FUNCTIONS

Muladhara rules all feelings and beliefs contributing to the knowledge of safety and security. The primary belief governing this chakra is the belief that you are worthy of existing.

This chakra processes all primal feelings, including the five basic ones—anger, sadness, fear, disgust, and joy—and related survival reactions, including rage, resentment, futility, despair, terror, abandonment, rejection, shame, guilt, bliss, oneness, and longing. When beliefs—usually created in response to experiences in the family-of-origin system—support your identity as a spiritual being, you can easily manifest money, love, a desirable career, and optimum physical health. If your eternal identity is compromised, such as by believing yourself unwanted, undeserving, and unworthy, your primary survival needs are also compromised. As a result, as you mature you might experience insufficient finances, inadequate primary relationships, an unhappy career, and more.

As I shared earlier in this chapter, this chakra encompasses your earliest childhood issues in this life but also karma and dharma from past lives. Together, these components determine the happiness or unhappiness of your current life. You are also responsible for creating karma as you go; this is called prarabdha karma. From a Hindu perspective, the way to form positive karma or dharma is by learning how to control your *manas*, or mind, as well as your senses, through discipline (*sadhana*).

Within this mix, kundalini stirs to life all seeds, activating the positive and negative to illuminate your emotional and mental programs so you can work on them as they develop throughout your life.

Common traumas related to the first chakra include being exposed to sexual or physical abuse or addictions, money challenges, birthing complications, abandonment, and not being wanted. Other traumas can include being exposed to war, genocide, violence, ethnic or religious discrimination, bullying, and more.

What happens if this chakra is emotionally disturbed? There are many psychological symptoms, including lack of safety, security, and trust; inability to manifest; lack of connection to home or primary relationships; disconnection from societal norms; lack of groundedness; and depression, anxiety, or addictions. Someone with psychological imbalances in the first chakra can also be deeply hurt, resentful, or filled with hate and blame toward others.

PSYCHOLOGICAL DEFICIENCIES IN AN UNHEALTHY FIRST CHAKRA

If your first chakra is out of balance psychologically, you might display any number of problems. The overriding issue will be feeling insecure and unable to trust the world, other people, or yourself. You might lack vitality or an excitement for life and be either completely unmotivated toward success or, conversely, overly motivated. The latter personality trait indicates a lack of belief in innate safety, so there is a perceived need to attempt to force it into being.

Additional symptoms include being spacey and disconnected; being underweight; fear and anxiety; lack of focus or follow-through; self-destructiveness; the sense of being unlovable; masochistic or suicidal tendencies; passivity; financial lack; and poor boundaries. You might also simply sense that you don't belong anywhere and strive excessively to please others—or you do the opposite because what's the point?

Other challenges can include overeating and being overweight; greed, hoarding, and excessive materiality;

hypochondria; paranoia; excessive spending; laziness and fatigue; fear of change; obsession with security; and rigid boundaries.

PSYCHOLOGICAL STRENGTHS IN THE HEALTHY FIRST CHAKRA

If your first chakra is balanced, you'll enjoy physical ease, security, and prosperity. You can work toward goals and still put your feet up at night. You'll also employ common sense (which isn't all that common) and hold reasonable expectations about the time and resources needed to achieve your goals.

You'll experience your body as pleasurable but not overdo the basics. Everything in moderation, right? This includes eating, drinking, exercising, getting outdoors, and being sexual. As well, you'll be known as reliable, motivated, and adventurous.

ASSOCIATED ARCHETYPES

An archetype is a template or a model. The positive archetype associated with the first chakra is the Mother. This archetype represents maternal sympathy, the magical feminine authority, reason being informed by spirituality, helpful instincts, and everything that cherishes, sustains, and fosters growth.

Muladhara's negative archetype is that of Victim. The Victim archetype alerts us to the possibility of being used for another's gain but can also make us feel too disempowered to face our issues.

PERSONALITY PROFILE

Certain people are very gifted in the first chakra. This means that they prefer to operate from this energy center, whether they choose to do so consciously or unconsciously. Does that description fit you? I'll fill you in on the personality traits associated with the first chakra so you can evaluate.

A strong root chakra person is very physically oriented and loves what the physical world has to offer. Their main objective is to meet their own primary needs, especially those related to material concerns. They then turn to the concerns of others.

They feel successful when making a difference in the everyday world, such as through building or creating tangible resources and services. The balanced first chakra person has strong character and tremendous stamina, following their passion to better the tangible world.

If you are this person, make sure you balance your desires for material gain with an ethical tool kit that allows success for all, not just yourself.

THE INTUITIVE GIFT
OF THE FIRST CHAKRA

When we're born, the first chakra is automatically available to perform physical empathy. This is the ability to sense information coming from others' bodies in your own body. For instance, when your first chakra is tuned in, you might feel another's knee pain in your own knee.

This aptitude is exceptionally helpful when someone else needs your attention. Imagine that a child or pet is crying and can't tell you what is wrong. With this extraordinary psychic intelligence, you might be able to tell that they have a cold or a pinched nerve.

The downside of this attribute is that it isn't always easy to sort your own physical problem or need from another's. Are you really craving that ice cream or is that your friend's desire? Using this gift is more beneficial if you figure out what is your own versus someone else's physical sensation. The following short practice will help you do this.

WHAT IS YOUR PHYSICAL EMPATHIC SIGN RATHER THAN ANOTHER'S?

If your body is sending you a physical signal, such as a pain, desire, craving, or ill feeling, take a few deep breaths and relax. Then set your attention on your first chakra in the hip area. Attune consciously to the physical event and ask yourself this question: *Is this my own physical sensation?*

Now pay attention to the rising of your energy in your body. If you feel electricity lifting from your first chakra and upward into your spine, the physical impression is your own and you want to pay attention to it. That energy will feel warm, uplifting, and pleasing. If the electrical energy falls downward and into your legs instead, the symptoms belong to someone else. You'll feel a decreased vitality in your overall constitution, a chill, and depression. If the energy seems to belong to someone else, request that your inner self send it back to them for processing, thus relieving your first chakra of that stress.

SUMMARY

Events from this and other lifetimes program your first chakra psychologically. They determine your fundamental sense of safety and security in the world. In turn, these beliefs can affect your experience in the material world as well as your ability to meet or enjoy the fundamental physicality you're in this body to enjoy. Employing your innate physical empathy—the ability to sense what is happening in the external world—can assist you in reading others to your own and their advantage, even as you continue the path of earth-star enjoyment.

Ready to put all this knowledge to work? Part 2 will do just that.

PART 2

APPLYING FIRST CHAKRA
KNOWLEDGE IN REAL LIFE

• • • • • •

Get ready for a deep dive into your root chakra and everything you can gain through your interactions with it. Each of the following chapters is written by a different energy expert, and my prediction is that you'll revisit these chapters over and over again. After all, your earth-star chakra is fundamental to all levels of your well-being. Life is in continual motion, and that constant change calls for a need to revisit the power-packed chakra that combines the grounding activity of the earth element with the rocket fuel of the stars.

You can read the chapters in part 2 in any order you choose. If you sense that learning about shapes will best enable your growth when it comes to the first chakra, turn to Gina Nicole's chapter about colors and shapes. Are you selecting a gemstone to assist you in getting a raise? Margaret Ann Lembo's chapter on that subject will call you like a siren. Think a meal that is supportive of your first chakra will give you some zip and zap? It's true! Turn to the recipe chapter.

To help you make excellent use of the information and practices contained in this part, I am going to first share something about intention and help you ground your first chakra—and *then* you can start playing!

YOU'LL BE USING INTENTION

To experience your desired life, you must focus on your desires. *Intention* is the code word for bringing dreams into reality. It occurs when you bring your conscious, unconscious, and subconscious thoughts and feelings to bear on a creative urge. This basic principle is at the heart of most universal laws, including the laws of physics.

We use intention all the time every day, even if we're not aware of it. If you rise in the morning with a sense of dismay, you'll perceive the day's events with dread. It will be hard for anything that happens to appear beneficial. But if you seize control of your attitude and decide that you'll notice all the blessings that greet you or that you provide for others, you'll meet your experiences with a positive mood that will prove itself accurate.

The easiest way to set an intention is to compose a statement of desire. There are three basic parts to that formula. The first is to establish a dream or need and phrase it in the present time. As well, make sure you keep this aspect of the statement uplifting and positive.

The second step is to feel that outcome you desire as if it is already happening. The third is to remind yourself about this decision as often as you need to, for yes, it is a full-on decision, not a wishy-washy idea. If necessary, tie that resolution into any timing involved. For instance, if you need to get something done by the end of the day, insert that choice into the intention.

Let's try it.

Think about something you'd like that relates to your first chakra. Money? Sex? Housing? A career opportunity? Physical health? Making a conscientious choice about food? Now form that interest into a present-tense statement. Following is an example.

I am making healthy choices about food and exercise.

Do you want to hold this focus for only one day? That's okay. Change occurs a day at a time. You could add this phrase.

*I am making healthy choices about food
and exercise for this entire day.*

Before fully committing to this intention, run it through your whole body. Since it involves your first chakra, you could start there. Embrace this intention within the entirety of your first chakra. Picture red, the color of that chakra, or any other that strikes your fancy, and illuminate it throughout your subtle and physical bodies. Then anchor this intention as a decision.

That's right. You have now decided to make this intention true, and it shall be so.

GROUNDING YOUR FIRST CHAKRA

Grounding is a process that involves anchoring your first chakra in the earth and assuring that you have access to it whenever you need it. This is a great exercise to walk through before conducting any of the practices in the upcoming chapters; they will take effect more swiftly and powerfully if you do this exercise first. It also uses concepts from the Hindu tradition to root you in history as well as in your future.

In a meditative state, move through this process:

While either standing or sitting, imagine a beam of light, called a grounding cord, traveling from the top of your head through the base of your spine into the center of the earth. Now picture a white light from the heavens entering the cord at the top of your head. This white light enters the grounding cord and surrounds and enfolds it.

This heavenly energy now uses the grounding cord to wash all impurities, toxins, and unnecessary energies into the center of the earth, which will transmute them through its fiery nature. Once you feel cleansed by the light, allow your spirit—your higher self—to determine which earth elements will best nourish, sustain, and empower your physical and energetic bodies.

You might sense an incoming flow of any number of nature elements: earth, water, air, metal, or fire. Notice a resulting sense of being present, calm, and renewed.

While in this state of serenity, concentrate for a moment on each of the four promises Hindu sacred scripture has revealed. These constitute your birthright for spiritual development:

THE RIGHT TO THINK AND REFLECT (MANANA). Ask the Divine what you need to reflect upon in this moment and what you are supposed to do with the resulting awareness.

THE RIGHT TO MAKE POSITIVE RESOLUTIONS (SANKALPA). What intentions do you need to set? What resolution will reflect your identity?

THE RIGHT TO REMOVE DOUBTS (VIKALPA). What false ideas can the Divine help you release or transform? What doubts—about your own lovability, worthiness, and giftedness—are you ready to release?

THE RIGHT TO BE AWARE OF YOUR OWN DIVINE SELF (ATMA CHINTANA). Ask the Divine to help you pinpoint, embrace, and expand your own true self, now and forevermore.

Take a few breaths and ask your true self to continue accepting the cleansing flow of heavenly white light, as well as the uplifting support of the earth, for as long as needed. Now smile and let this firm grounding in your first chakra lead you into your day.

4

SPIRIT ALLIES

MARGARET ANN LEMBO

Spirit allies are available to everyone. They take many forms, and we all have an entourage of these energetic assistants for all aspects of life—invisible helpers that show up upon request. You can feel the essence of these helpers on a vibrational level. Communication with spirit allies is most often telepathic: mind-to-mind and heart-to-heart communication using thoughts, feelings, and visualization.

Spirit allies can be angels and archangels, plant spirits, animal guides, the fairies and other natural forces related to essential oils, and more.

ANGELS AND ARCHANGELS, ANIMAL GUIDES, AND FAIRY AND OTHER NATURAL FORCES

For as long as I can remember, angels have been part of my daily life. As a child, I felt and saw them in my imagination, and I called on their help whenever I was afraid or needed guidance. I also knew as a young child that plants have energy and vibrate with consciousness. My interest in the teachings of nature, plants, and animals started in the garden with my mother. Thanks to the time I spent talking to and listening to the plants and flowers, my attunement to a spiritually rich life also grew in the garden.

If we are open to it, it can be easy to link telepathically with all life. Spirit allies are always divinely influencing us, and we are always receiving guidance from all of nature for our contemplation. The seen and unseen are both real worlds, and the unseen beings and energies help guide and light our path.

The root chakra is the chakra of vitality, endurance, and sexual energy. Do you need some help overcoming procrastination? Bringing balance to your first chakra with the help of your spirit allies can put an end to procrastination. Work with spirit allies whenever you have a task at hand that requires focus and mental endurance for successful completion.

Two more qualities of the root chakra are steadfastness and diligence. Through this chakra, you can activate your passion for living and release feelings of apathy. Keywords for the root chakra are grounding, health, money, nutrition, protection, and safety.

Just as a tree has roots deep in the earth to keep it firmly planted, so are the roots of your own thoughts and beliefs stored within the root chakra at the base of your spine. This chakra is all about the physical part of your life, which includes a safe place to live, healthy food to eat, and good water to drink. The root chakra is also the part of you that learns to earn and save money, as well as how to spend it wisely.

I've provided descriptions of allies to connect with to commit to a goal, including affirmations you can use to work with each ally.

Affirmations are empowering statements that employ intention. As Cyndi explored in her opening remarks in part 2, intention employs your inner powers to help a dream come true. With intention, you can also create a bond between yourself and an ally and use that relationship to strengthen a desire.

When set into an affirmation, an intention such as "I am now connecting with an angel" will bring that angel to you and assist you in recognizing their presence. If you were to use a phrase like "An angel is giving me a sign," you are basically opening yourself to receiving a message from an angel. Affirmations activate our intuition, draw supportive guides to us, and help us be aware of actions we must take to bring about the types of wishes linked to our first chakra, such as the meeting of fundamental needs and relationships. Enjoy the affirmations I've suggested for each type of spirit guide and feel free to also create your own.

ANGELS AND ARCHANGELS

Angels and archangels are androgynous: neither masculine nor feminine. While humankind has personified them to look like humans with wings and flowing robes, they are actually beings of light, color, and vibration. They aren't just available for spiritual requests, either. Your very real root chakra desires—such as money, loving relationships, physical health, and fortitude—are quite important to these encouraging beings. What is important to us in our everyday lives is also important to them.

Angels act and react based on the thoughts of their human charges. They respond to prayers, requests, and petitions. Upon request they act as divine messengers, communicating guidance and wisdom and orchestrating synchronicity, based on divine will and the highest good of all concerned. The key to working with angels and archangels is to remember to ask for their assistance.

Your Guardian Angel

Your guardian angel is always available to you. Here is a simple traditional prayer from my childhood that you can use to request your guardian angel's assistance:

Angel of the Divine, my guardian dear, to whom
infinite love commits you here. Ever this day be
at my side to light and guard, to rule and guide.
Guardian angel, please come and help me!

AFFIRMATIONS: I know I always have an angel at my
side. I am grateful that angels light my path and
inspire me. I can handle any situation that arises
in relationship to my root chakra. I appreciate the
support available to me in all areas of my life.

Angel of Action

The root chakra is the energy center where you store your
ability to take action and move forward. When you need
to move past perceived blocks, call on the Angel of Action.
When you feel stymied and frustrated with your progress,
either generally in your life or with regard to a specific
project, the Angel of Action can help get things flowing
and motivate you to take a step—any step—toward your
intended goal. Request that the Angel of Action help you
gain clarity on the reason you feel as you do, refocus your
attention and imagination on your goal or the completion
of it, and lead you to the information or resources you need
so you can take action.

AFFIRMATIONS: Everything I need or want is always
available to me. Love, wealth, and plenitude come

naturally to me. I have plenty of money and plenty to share. Blessings are constantly flowing into my life.

Angel of Physical Strength

The root chakra is the energetic location of physical strength and a healthy foundation. Ask yourself: "Do I feel physically strong?" Call on the Angel of Physical Strength when you feel your endurance is lacking and you tire easily. With this angel by your side, you can find the motivation you need to take the action required to strengthen your core and improve your physical endurance. Ask this angel to guide you to the right activities for your body type to improve your physical structure.

> **AFFIRMATIONS:** My energy is balanced. My physical structure is strong. I get sufficient sunlight to maintain a healthy body. I move my body and exercise regularly. My physical vitality and endurance are increasing. My body is rock solid.

Angel of Abundance and Prosperity

Call on the Angel of Abundance and Prosperity when you perceive a deficiency in some first chakra aspect of your life. Your root chakra encompasses your basic material needs and also the desire for extra resources, such as time and money. Uncover why you feel you don't have enough or there isn't plenty for you and those around you. Be as specific as possible. Once you've identified the lack, call on the Angel of Abundance and Prosperity to help you see how you can improve the situation.

> **AFFIRMATIONS:** I am grateful for the abundance, ease, and prosperity in my life. I enjoy my loyal and supportive friends and family. Everything I need or want is always available to me.

Archangel Ariel

Archangel Ariel is a protector and healer. This archangel can aid in aligning your focus with doing what it takes to improve your first chakra vitality and vigor on all levels, including your mental and emotional states. Call on Ariel when you want to be more proactive in health-promoting and rejuvenating activities. Archangel Ariel helps increase motivation and is available to guide you to trust your intuitive realizations and give you the courage to act upon that knowledge. Call on Ariel to amplify your core strength on all levels, especially physically. Ariel is also your ally to motivate you to take the action necessary to increase your financial well-being.

> **AFFIRMATIONS:** I am healthy, whole, and complete. It is safe for me to shine my light brightly. I am self-confident and grateful. I recognize my self-worth. It is easy for me to set boundaries.

Archangel Thuriel

Archangel Thuriel is the guardian of animals and helps interspecies connection, specifically among humans and animals. This is the archangel that will help encourage outdoor playtime in nature and with animals, important factors for a thriving first chakra. Archangel Thuriel is your guide to help you realize how interconnected all life is and that nature, plants, and animals are a major reason to be grateful.

> **AFFIRMATIONS:** It is easy for me to communicate
> with animals and plants. I am flexible. I enjoy
> spending time in nature.

ANIMAL GUIDES

Animal guides are available to all of us. After all, we are part of the natural world, that great cycle of life that ebbs and flows around us. An animal guide might be show up in 3D, such as through the citing of an actual animal, or visit psychically. Latter examples including an appearance in a dream or through an intuitive flash. Following are two samples of root chakra animals that might reach out to bring you a message or support the development of a strength.

Elk

Elk is an ally for strength, endurance, and sexual potency. When Elk migrates into your life, you can find comfort and great strength by sharing food with a group of people. The blessing of the community provides sustenance beyond the nutritional value of food. It is important to remember to feed your body, mind, and soul. How is your stamina? Do you feel healthy and strong? Elk's message is to recharge your energy centers, especially the root chakra, and renew your passion for living a vibrant life.

> **AFFIRMATIONS:** I am strong. My inner core is powerful. I am grateful for the support of my community. I am physically fit, mentally focused, and emotionally balanced. Vital life force flows vigorously through me, providing me with endurance.

Gorilla

Self-care and rest are important factors for maintaining balance on a root chakra level. As a guide, Gorilla is an ally when you need to learn to rest, relax, play, and take the time to socialize. When Gorilla struts into your life, it signals a time for regeneration and rejuvenation through healthy diet and social interaction in a restful way. Mother Earth wants to spend more time with you and feel your hands and feet upon her body, filling up your senses with her loving gifts. Investigate the use of nature's pharmacy, such as herbs and essential oils, for holistic health. Gift yourself with time to rejuvenate your physical body and your emotions.

AFFIRMATIONS: I am safe. My body is calm and relaxed. I sleep well and rejuvenate my body. Rest and relaxation are a regular part of my life.

FAIRY AND OTHER NATURAL FORCES

Nature is full of beings and forces that include us in her majesty. Some of these beings belong to the fairy realm, which is also called the deva kingdom. This is a special grouping of spirits that can be called to assist you in connecting to the energy in an herb, plant, or even an essential oil composed of a natural substance.

Essential oils can be made of a vast number of natural products, including flower petals and the parts of plants such as leaves, bark, roots, rinds, seeds, and more. There are many ways to work with an essential oil. I suggest you try all of them out to find your favorite.

One method is to drip a couple drops of an oil in a small container of a neutral carrier like almond oil. Basically, you want to dilute the oil so it's between one and five percent of a gel or oil. You can then apply the liquid topically.

You can inhale an oil directly or put a few drops in a bath or on a warm or cold compress. You can also smell an oil through the air by using a diffuser that disperses the oil. Simply follow the instructions provided by the diffuser manufacturer.

Also, be careful with oils! They can be harmful if you're allergic to a specific oil or use in a way that causes internal or external reactions. Always check with a doctor if you are dealing with challenges or using medicines that could cause a problem with an oil.

Cedarwood Essential Oil

Many cultures have used the smoke or scent of burning herbs or parts of plants for positive and healing effects, including certain Buddhist sects,[4] amongst the ancient Celts,[5] and by various Native American tribes, including the Lakota, the Ojibwa, and the First People of Canada. One source of ceremonial smoke is cedar, which is one of the four sacred

4   Admin_Higashi_USA, Reverend Ken Yamada, "Meaning of Incense," May 22, 2022, https://higashihonganjiusa.org/2020/05/22/meaning -of-incense/.

5   Scott, "Saining Is not Smudging," https://cailleachs-herbarium.com /2019/02/saining-not-smudging-purification-and-lustration-in -scottish-folk-magic-practice/.

medicines of the latter. It is used to replace negative energy with positive energy.[6]

Cedar is an evergreen tree that can grow to a height of over one hundred feet. Its essential oil is useful when you want to ground a prayer, meditation, or visualization practice. Inhale cedarwood oil to help you remember to ground yourself, which is a major function of the first chakra. Use it to replenish your focus when you are experiencing mental fatigue. Do you want to amplify your focus and ability to ground your spiritual experiences? Allow the qualities of cedarwood to amplify your focus and the preservation of knowledge, wisdom, love, and protection.

AFFIRMATION: With every step I take, I am aware of my connection with the sacred ground. The vibrant emerald-green energy of the plants and trees nurtures and restores my body, mind, and spirit.

FOR YOUR SAFETY: Do not use if you are pregnant or nursing.

6   Indigenous Inclusion Directorate, "Smudging protocol and guidelines for school divisions, 2019), The Government of Manitoba, https://www.edu.gov.mb.ca/iid/publications/pdf/smudging_guidelines.pdf.

Patchouli Essential Oil

Patchouli is a bushy, hairy-leafed herb that reaches heights of about three feet. It has light purple flowers and oblong leaves. The earthy scent of patchouli essential oil is grounding. It brings focus and promotes action, thereby releasing laziness. Patchouli's aroma increases your awareness of issues or challenges, allowing you to perceive them from a higher perspective and thereby increasing your objectivity and ability to see the bigger picture. Patchouli can also help you feel emotionally safe, as it strengthens your sense of self.

AFFIRMATION: I'm self-motivated to be productive. My tasks and creative projects are completed with ease. I am a caretaker of the earth, and I take the time to enjoy nature.

FOR YOUR SAFETY: Has a stimulant effect when used excessively and a sedative effect when used sparingly.

Sage Essential Oil

Sage is a Mediterranean evergreen plant that grows up to three feet tall. It has grayish-green leaves and small lavender-colored flowers. Inhale sage essential oil with the intention of shaking out emotional states that have been firmly established in the root chakra. Sage is beneficial for releasing negative thoughts and old, repetitive ways. It reduces anxiety, raises your vibration, and is especially helpful for feeling safe and protected, a key quality of a balanced root chakra.

> **AFFIRMATION:** I am safe and sound. I am out of harm's way. All is well. I surround myself with trustworthy people.

> **FOR YOUR SAFETY:** Could have adverse effects on the central nervous system if you use more than is present as a food seasoning. Do not use if you are pregnant or nursing.

Vetiver Essential Oil

Vetiver is a tropical grass that reaches a height of up to eight feet. The essential oil is extracted from the aromatic roots, which make it a perfect root chakra balancer. The musky, earthy fragrance is sure to support you when you need to maintain focus on the present moment. The energetic signature of vetiver essential oil aligns you with taking the time for rest and renewal. Vetiver is a perfect essential oil for connecting with elemental spirits, natural forces, and the fairy kingdom. It will also help you stay grounded during spiritual practices when used in very small amounts.

This is a perfect oil for earth-centered spiritual pursuit, earth-based rituals, and shamanic journeywork.

AFFIRMATION: I am grounded, focused, and energized. I have plenty of energy and time to accomplish what I need and want to get done.

SUMMARY

With focused intention and a little help from your spirit allies, you have the know-how to change unconscious influences into conscious intentions. Access your memory bank and uncover stored belief systems using angels, archangels, animals, and aromatherapy. These allies are important tools for becoming self-aware. They can help you uncover pent-up emotions and feelings that are stored in your body, mind, or spirit at any time when you are feeling blocked or heavy and don't know why.

Establishing intention and accessing the unlimited potential provided by your imagination are important components of working with this vibrational team.

5

YOGA POSES

AMANDA HUGGINS

Yoga was my first love—spiritually, at least. I was first drawn to the practice over a decade ago, admittedly with very little understanding of what yoga was truly about. All I knew was that other people seemed to enjoy it, and those other people seemed less stressed than I was. As an anxious, burnt-out professional, I was ready to try anything to cultivate a deeper sense of grounding and balance in my life.

I quickly learned that yoga is far more than just a trendy workout; it is an ancient and sacred practice that unites mindfulness, movement, and breath. Each *asana*—the traditional Sanskrit term for yoga postures—presents a new opportunity for union between your physical and energetic bodies. Whether flowing through multiple poses or holding the stillness of a singular posture, you're creating pathways to direct and move unseen energy of the subtle body through the physical body. No matter the pose, when you are mindfully present to the energy flowing throughout the physical body, you're practicing energy work on yourself. How cool is that?

I want to assure you that you do *not* need any prerequisites to receive the energetic benefits of yoga. A common misconception is that the practice requires immense flexibility, a specific body type, or a certain amount of physical capacity. Untrue!

Yoga—*true* yoga—is meant to be accessible to all, and I encourage you to dissolve any preconceived notions about yoga and physical ability. As long as you have a beating heart (and at least one good lung), you are already capable of the most "expert-level" yoga posture of all: breathing.

This chapter explores how you can utilize the practice of yoga to connect with your first chakra. I will offer postures and a simple yoga sequence you can practice in the comfort of your own home, as well as accessible postures for those experiencing physical conditions that limit movement.

The only requirement throughout this section is a sense of playful, open-hearted curiosity… and perhaps a water bottle.

YOGA AND THE FIRST CHAKRA

As you've learned by now, your root chakra is connected to your sense of stability and grounding: two qualities that directly translate onto the yoga mat. The word *yoga* originates from the Sanskrit root sound *yuj*, meaning to yoke or unite. When explored through the lens of the root chakra, you are joining breath and movement and creating emotional and energetic balance that will pay dividends in all aspects of life.

The first chakra is intricately connected with the autonomic nervous system's fight-or-flight response to stress. Because yoga integrates mind, body, and spirit, it offers an incredible playground to practice managing the nervous system. When a yogi intends to create energetic stability and balance in their root chakra, they are being challenged to create physical balance through the poses, emotional safety in the mind, and autonomic nervous system regulation through the breath.

When you pair deep, conscious breathing with yogic movement, you stimulate the parasympathetic nervous system. Not only does that enhance your sense of groundedness and stability during yoga poses, but over time it can develop greater balance within your autonomic nervous system. In other words, the more you practice grounding and stability on the yoga mat, the more that grounded, stable feeling will show up *off* the mat.

As you connect with your first chakra through yoga, keep in mind that it's less about what you do and more about *how* you do it. Take mountain pose *(tadasana)*, for example. It's a pose that many of us unconsciously practice every day because the pose is simply standing on two feet!

Here's a quick little mental exercise for you: take a moment to think back on the past week and try to count exactly how many times you found yourself standing up each day. It's nearly impossible, right? Between work, errands, social activities, and just walking in general, it may be difficult to come up with an exact number. What if I asked you to think about just one time you stood up instead? Out of the hundreds, if not thousands, of times you found yourself standing this week, are you able to recall just one distinct moment when you felt actively connected to the earth—when you remember cultivating feelings of balance, stability, and groundedness?

This is the essence of "it's not what you do; it's *how* you do it." Technically, your body may have passed through mountain pose many times, but was your *mind* present?

The key is to maintain awareness and stay present to how you're moving so you can receive the messages of the first chakra in each and every pose:

You are connected.

You are grounded.

You are safe.

You.

Are.

Here.

ACTIVATING THE FIRST CHAKRA IN YOGA

"Root to rise" is one of the favorite phrases I've picked up throughout my years of teaching yoga. It's a cue to offer students clear, concise direction, but I'm equally fond of the poetic visualization "root to rise" creates.

Join me in the following brief root-to-rise exercise.

PRACTICE

ENERGETIC ACTIVATION OF THE FIRST CHAKRA

» On the ground or your yoga mat, with your feet hip-width distance apart, bend forward at the hips into a standing forward fold. If standing is not currently accessible, you can also take a forward fold from a chair.

» Keep the weight in the heels and bend the knees as much as needed to fold safely. There's no need to straighten the legs completely!

» Find depth in the pose by allowing the weight of your torso to pour down toward the earth.

» Stay here for a few cycles of breaths, deepening the fold with every exhale.

» Still in the fold, draw your attention to your first chakra. Envision threads of light stretching down from your root and through the thighs, knees, and feet, and see those roots move into the earth below you. You are connected.

» Now root to rise. Maintain that energetic connection with the earth and allow a powerful, grounded inhale to bring you to a standing position.

Did you feel that? There's a marked difference in the energy, power, and space created when you make the choice to ground from the first chakra.

Physically, the root chakra is related to the lower body: your lower back, glutes, legs, and feet. And because the lower body is connected to the earth in nearly every yoga posture, you have infinite opportunities to activate this energy center!

This can be done using simple, unembellished postures (like the standing forward fold you just practiced) or more challenging ones that test both body and mind (like tree pose, a one-legged posture that takes "root to rise" to new heights). Regardless of the shapes your body is making, the fundamentals of *how* to connect with the root chakra will remain the same.

Physical Fundamentals

Your feet are the foundation for alignment. Creating a solid physical foundation triggers a chain of energetic events. First, placing focus creates balance and equal weight distribution in the feet. Then that energy travels up through the lower legs, quads, and glutes, engaging whichever muscles are necessary for the pose. With the lower body sturdy and supported, the mid and upper spine can elongate, creating room in the body for deep, spacious breath.

That may sound like a lot to remember, but the body has a fantastic way of intuitively knowing what to do. If all else fails, just remember to *FEEL:*

F—Feet plant into the mat.

E—Envision your roots.

E—Energy flows through the first chakra.

L—Lose your balance.

Yes, lose your balance! Wobbling or falling out of a pose is to be expected. The intent with first chakra activation is not to create perfect stillness in the shapes. Rather, it's to cultivate a sense of inner stability, especially in the moments when you feel unstable. Not only is losing balance a natural part of the practice, but there's deep wisdom to be found in exploring how you treat yourself *after* losing balance. Practicing stability and grounding is nothing without compassion and kind inner dialogue!

CHILD'S POSE

Ready to employ yoga to connect with and activate your first chakra? Through this practice, I'm going to introduce you to child's pose. This is an ideal activity to enhance your first chakra and prepare for the next practice, which will kick off with child's pose and then present a sequence of first chakra yoga poses. You'll enjoy enlivening your root chakra so you can connect with the earth and reach for the stars.

Kneel on the floor or a yoga mat and rest your seat atop your heels. Keep your toes together and space your knees hip-width apart. Set your palms atop your thighs and take a few deep, healing breaths with your eyes closed. Envision first chakra activation and feel your roots connecting with and drawing energy from the earth. Perhaps offer yourself the mantra "I am safe."

Next, on an exhale, lower your torso between your knees. Extend your arms down your torso and keep your palms facing downward. Relax your shoulders so it feels like they are connecting energetically to the ground. You can remain in this position as long as it's comfortable.

Modifications: If you are unable to find child's pose, any comfortable seated position is fine, such as a seated pose. (You can choose between these based on comfort level.) Sit on the ground or a mat with feet crossed over the legs or not. Simply breathe deeply and imagine a grounding cord linking your first chakra with the earth.

PRACTICE

YOGA FLOW TO AWAKEN AND STRENGTHEN THE FIRST CHAKRA

Our root chakra greatly benefits by the performance of a yoga sequence, or a series of yoga poses done right after each other. The following sequence will help you cultivate a sense of grounding and stability.

» begin in child's pose

» rise to a tabletop position for cat and cow pose

With both hands and knees firmly planted on the ground, take three to five rounds of cat and cow pose: drop the low belly on your inhales for cow pose, and as you exhale, "cat" the spine—draw the upper spine toward the sky and drop the head. Throughout this, maintain the stable connection with your first chakra.

Modification: If you'd like to sit in a chair, do so, with your seat slightly forward so that both feet are firmly on the ground and close to each other. Set your hands on your knees and slightly arch your back, keeping your neck straight as you look forward. Then exhale and curl your spine and push your palms slightly away from you, although they will remain on your knees. As you inhale, flatten your back again and sit tall. You may deepen the stretch by interlacing both hands and extending them out in front of you with palms facing away from the body as you exhale.

» downward-facing dog

Starting on all fours, find downward-facing dog for a few cycles of breath. Press into your hands and feet as you extend your legs while keeping your back and arms straight. Draw energy from the feet, up the legs, and into the root chakra on your inhales. Use the exhales to sink your roots deeper into the earth. Find stability.

Modification: You may skip downward-facing dog altogether if mobility is limited. Instead, practice seated inhalations and exhalations. As you breathe in, draw the arms up to the sky to find length. As you breathe out, bring hands to your heart center, palms together. Find the balance and stability here.

» low lunge

From down dog, step the right foot in between the hands and settle the left knee down onto the mat. As you inhale, lift torso and arms to the sky. Stay for three to five cycles of breath. You may find yourself wobbly here—that's wonderful! Use every delicious wobble as a cue to root down more. Steady the breath and release. Repeat on the other side.

Modification: You may substitute with gentle seated twists. Inhale to bring arms to the sky; exhale to drop left hand to right knee. Repeat on the other side.

» return to downward-facing dog

Take a moment to collect information from the body. What feels different? Are you breathing? As you return to inner stillness, offer the mantra "I am grounded."

» warrior 2

Step the right foot in between both hands. Drop the back left heel down and angle the toes to point slightly toward the front of your mat. Press the four corners of your feet down, and root to rise. Inhale and raise the arms parallel to the floor, with shoulders down and neck long. Stay here for three to five cycles of breath. With every inhale, draw length and strength up through the root chakra; with every exhale, create more grounding as you drop deeper into the pose. Repeat on left side.

Modification: You may substitute with gentle seated twists. Inhale to bring arms to the sky. As you exhale, bring arms parallel with the ground and twist to the left. Repeat on the other side.

> » return to downward-facing dog
> » walk hands toward your feet and find
>   a forward fold at the back of your mat

Just as we did in the earlier exercise, find a deep sense of grounding and activation from feet to first chakra. Take deep, healing breaths as you drop your weight forward toward the earth. Trust that you are grounded. Stay here for three to five breath cycles.

Modification: For a seated forward fold, sit forward on your chair and breathe deeply. Extend your spine as you fold your upper body over your legs. You can either let your arms drop naturally to your side or keep your hands on your thighs and use them for extra support as you fold over comfortably. When ready, lift your torso back up into an upright position.

» rise to standing

Take a large inhale and rise to stand, extending the arms up overhead. As you exhale, draw hands to heart center in prayer. Allow the eyes to close and once more draw awareness to your energy center. You may stay here as long as you'd like, softly exploring any fluctuations in balance.

Modification: Find a tall spine from your seat and hold your hands loosely in your lap.

» repeat entire flow twice more

On the last and final standing pose, offer yourself and the earth beneath you a moment of gratitude.

» savasana

Close the practice by lying on the floor with the palms facing up. Allow the earth beneath you to support the entirety of your body weight. Let the breath's natural rhythm arise. You may choose to envision the color red as you softly breathe, rest, and restore. Stay here for as long as you'd like.

Modification: Seated savasana. Allow the eyes to close and the palms to softly rest in your lap. Let go of any tension in the body and simply receive the restorative benefits of relaxation.

» close with a mantra

When you are ready, open your eyes. You may bring your hands to touch your body (at heart's center or on the low belly). Close with the mantra "I am here."

I encourage you to use your movement practice to explore what works for *you*. Allow the poses to feel spacious and empowering, and allow yourself to connect (and reconnect) with your first chakra, the earth, and your inner self as you journey along.

SUMMARY

In many yoga classes, we close with a simple acknowledgement of *namaste*: "The light in me recognizes the light in you." I sincerely hope the brilliant red light of your first chakra shines bright within you, and that you cast that beautiful glow onto those around you!

6

BODY WISDOM

NITIN BHATNAGAR, DO

Physicians do not often discuss the chakras. The concept seems alien to most professionals in the field of traditional medicine, who aren't usually exposed to or trained in alternative or holistic health care modalities. Yet chakra healing has been integral to ancient medicine spanning many cultures across the globe.

As a practicing clinical cardiologist, I believe chakra medicine can only aid us in our healing work. After all, too often modern medicine offers more bandages than cures. My goal in this chapter is to help bridge the worlds of traditional medicine and alternative healing practices by exploring the physicality of the body via energetic medicine. I'll even delve into the body-mind connections that science has found to be vital to our well-being and provide exercises for increasing all levels of your health through your first chakra.

THE BEAUTY OF THE PHYSICAL
FROM THE UNIVERSE TO THE CHAKRAS

The universe is beautifully designed, as is yet another creation of exquisite perfection: the human body. Just as the manifest universe is made of energy vibrating at different frequencies, so too is the body.

Many scientific inquiries regard the universe as holographic in nature, made up of light traveling at varying frequencies throughout the cosmos. When that light reaches a certain level of density, it slows down and creates an atomic structure that at its core is still a vibrating solid.

This phenomenon applies to all living cells in the body. Cells communicate with each other, and these connections expand into complex structures. They then organize into various systems, including the nervous, cardiovascular, endocrine, gastric, and immune systems, and many others. Their respective organs also form communication centers that operate like highways throughout the body, such as the bloodstream and the lymphatic vessels. Yet fundamentally, all cells and organ systems are simply energies moving in varying degrees of vibrational states.

The dense body is also accompanied by energy centers known as chakras. Within the confines of the chakras lie every memory and every experience—past, present, and future—in the form of pure energy. Yes, you read that correctly: the future as well. Fundamentally, everyone seeking improvement in the body must see the universe and everything and everyone in it as composed of energy. This energy exists in all time and space dimensions and yet transcends them all, as is presently being explored through the field of quantum physics.

Each chakra regulates specific aspects of our lives. It also evolves alongside us while serving as a biofeedback mechanism. For example, if an area of the body is ridden with illness, the related chakra might be affected as well. When a chakra is affected, the body can manifest the corresponding host of illnesses. So the cause of an issue—as well as the solution—can be discovered by exploring the body and its associated chakras.

As you learned earlier in the book, each chakra corresponds to an associated gland. The first or root chakra is associated with the adrenal glands. This chakra interacts with the adrenals in the same way everything does: energetically.

Consider a light bulb. Once it is turned on, electrical energy is transmitted in the form of light to fill the room. In the same way, the first chakra's energetic vibrations shine upon all corresponding body parts, including the organs and their associated hormones.

FIRST CHAKRA ANATOMY AND
BASIC PHYSICAL FUNCTION

To really benefit from interactions with your first chakra, it's helpful to have a broad understanding of its relationship to your anatomy. We will be revisiting some of the material from part 1 here, but I believe the reinforcement will be useful in painting a clear picture so you can derive powerful benefits from your work with the first chakra.

Every chakra is anchored at a key location within the body. Your first chakra is situated at the base of the spinal column, between the root of the reproductive organs and the anus. It relates to the sacrococcygeal nerve plexus at the end of the spinal cord. Here the fibrous tissue of the filum terminale passes from the conus medullaris and supports the spinal cord.

Your filum terminale is a fibrous band that helps buffer and stabilize your spinal cord. The conus medullaris is the end of the spine and is located around the first lumbar vertebra. Interlapping with the conus medullaris is the cauda equina, a group of nerve roots and nerves that occupy the first through fifth vertebrae of the spine. An extensive network of nerves continues from the cauda equina to branch down through the second sacral vertebra and the coccygeal area. From here, it arouses activity in the hips, perineum, and bladder, before continuing to affect the nerves all the way into the feet.

The importance of the area involving the conus medullaris and cauda equina was known to the ancient Hindus. As Cyndi explored in part 1, this region of the body is called the kanda body, and it is considered the true home of the first chakra and the red kundalini. You can see how perfectly situated your first chakra is as the primary regulator of physical and survival energies, which in turn support security and safety.

The first chakra's associated gland, the adrenals, are your primary stress glands. They create hormonal shifts in response to internal and external stresses, running the rest of the body's functioning organ systems. The major adrenal hormones are steroidal, including adrenaline, cortisol, aldosterone, DHEA, and hydrocortisone.

When your adrenals are stimulated—for instance, when you are scared—these hormones cause your heart rate to rise. They also stir the nervous and musculoskeletal systems to get ready for fight or flight, whether the threat is an external physical one or just a thought in your mind.

Our adrenals will respond to an extensive list of stressors, whether perceived as positive or negative. *Any* threat to our safety and security—involving our health, work, relationships, or any other life-related matters—is met with an adrenal response. Even disturbances in our mood or feelings can stimulate a stress reaction.

Inflammatory or allergy-inducing foods can also lead to adrenal challenges and eventually chronic adrenal fatigue. So can deficiencies in vitamins B, C, D, and E, as well as low sodium, potassium, and magnesium levels.

HOW YOUR FIRST CHAKRA AFFECTS YOUR PHYSICAL BODY

We've touched on how the physical structures associated with the first chakra work in your body. The other side of the coin also affects your life: the state of your first chakra influences the physical functions of the bodily area it relates to.

For instance, if this chakra is working overtime, too much of its energy will be shot into your subtle and bodily systems, and in turn, your adrenal organs will be taxed.

If the chakra is under-functioning, your physical system won't have enough subtle or physical energy to draw from. You might not have enough energy to perform your life tasks or deal with emotions as they arise.

When you're experiencing challenges in the physical area of the first chakra or with related life concerns, it's sometimes hard to figure out which came first: did your first chakra cause the body to manifest illness or did the body's disease shift the energetics and alignment of the chakra?

I always recommend that you employ traditional medicine if you are nervous about what's happening. (After all, I'm a physician!) If you choose to make use of energy medicine practices, remain in contact with your allopathic physician to make sure you are meeting your health needs on all levels. Your first chakra and your body are not separate but are part of a well-oiled machine. The whole picture must be observed.

YOUR BODY AND MIND

Let's return to our discussion of the nervous system to focus on an incredibly important part of the formula for first chakra health: the mind.

When our psychology is out of balance, our physiology reacts to restore our state of authenticity and integrity. If we ignore our psychological needs, we'll never achieve wellness. In an attempt to bring balance, our internal chemistry will get so out of whack that we can easily become vulnerable to disease or illness.

Energetically, psychological factors—including our mindsets, judgments, and all feelings—compose subtle and physical information that is transmitted via our nervous system to all organ systems. If we fail to deal with the so-called negative factors such as fears and resentments, our health will be adversely affected. If we allow ourselves to focus on the more positive qualities, such as peace and love, our health will benefit.

I'll give you an example regarding thoughts. Thoughts might start as subtle energies, but they are then sent up and down the spinal cord through the nervous system, which is one of the main systems related to the first chakra. Our body will manifest either health or disease depending on the vibrational frequency of a certain thought or group of thoughts. Low, dense frequencies mitigate disease formation within the body, and higher, lighter frequencies create health.

When our nervous system gets blocked with low, dense frequencies, all subtle energy centers can be negatively affected, but each chakra has a specialty related to it. Specifically, our first chakra houses imbalanced, low frequencies related to infatuation, anger, pride, shame, resentments, and primary emotions. The vibrations will affect the adrenals and all parts of the body along the nerve pathways. Quite literally, severe stress can make us lose our footing because of the first chakra's relationship to our spine and adrenals—and, as we noted during our anatomical discussion, our feet. That's why a system overload under stress can make us stumble and fall.

In the end, the body holds the wisdom of our mind and experiences, while our chakras regulate the flow of energies. Among all the chakras, the root chakra is necessary for creating vitality, security, and physical well-being.

WORKING WITH FIRST CHAKRA ISSUES

How do you know if you are experiencing first chakra issues? What are some ways to deal with them? Let's take a look!

Do You Have First Chakra Issues?

Following is a list of conditions that might uncover this chakra as the origin of your presenting problems:

- » lower backaches
- » craving for sugar or salt
- » racing heart without exercise
- » a state of constant anxiety
- » perpetual tiredness
- » sense of being constantly victimized
- » an eating disorder
- » anxiety that might lead to panic
- » challenges in any of the first chakra systems or bodily parts explored in part 1, such as hip, rectum, or anus problems

A FEW EASY WAYS TO SUPPORT YOUR FIRST CHAKRA

BOXED BREATHING: This breathing exercise is something you can turn to throughout the day, whenever you have a spare moment. Inhale for a count of 4, 5, or 6 seconds (whatever feels right for you). Then hold the breath for the same number of seconds. Exhale for the same number of seconds, and at the bottom of the exhale hold the breath for that same duration. Repeat for a few breaths. This breathing exercise helps free you from insecurity, bringing feelings of safety by altering the balance of electrostatic forces.

FIRST CHAKRA FOODS: To assist your first chakra, I also recommend eating earthy foods, such as tomatoes, carrots, parsnips, potatoes, beets, onions, nuts, and berries. These deliver plenty of vitamins and minerals that are supportive of your adrenals.

COLOR THERAPY: Since the root chakra is associated with the color red, wearing red clothes can help boost your first chakra energies.

NOTE YOUR EMOTIONS: The root chakra is associated with a number of emotions, so it is helpful to keep a journal of your emotions, such as fear, sadness, joy, anger, and guilt.

PRACTICE

GROUNDING FOR
FIRST CHAKRA HEALTH

Your root chakra is well named. Your divine self and available spiritual energies need a spot where they can be rooted into the body and the earth. That's why grounding helps with first chakra healing. Grounding brings balance to the mind and body by "rooting the spirit."

One method I employ to ground myself is to walk barefoot through the grass in my backyard. Walking barefoot (when possible) is key, as this allows you to release your body's stressful positive ions into the earth. In high concentrations, positive ions are detrimental to our health. On the other hand, negative ions nurture health, and walking barefoot lets you absorb the peaceful negative ions emanated from the earth. Walking on grass or sand is best, but just getting outside can be helpful. Let the earth's endless supply of negative ions reduce inflammation and lower cortisol levels, speed up healing, relieve pain, and improve the quality of your sleep.[7]

---

7   Healthline, "The Effect of Negative Ions," https://www.healthline.com/health/negative-ions.

Another grounding practice is to immerse yourself in a nice warm salt bath at the end of the day. It's a great way to discharge those positive ions.

Himalayan salt lamps also get rid of those pesky positive ions. I have one in every room and hallway in the house.

Other grounding exercises include enjoying memory games, laughing out loud, using the left side of the brain by practicing logical mathematics, and getting involved with physical movement, such as through a sport. Even walking or stretching will do it.

THE MULADHARA MUDRA

There is a special mudra (hand gesture) that can assist in grounding your internal first chakra energies. Hand mudras are a special feature of tantric Buddhism and are also used in Indian classical dance. Medieval hatha yoga texts, which share physical yoga activities, are a major source of information about mudras.[8] It is called the Muladhara mudra, and it can be helpful to start and end the day with this practice. You can see the illustration in figure 2.

---

8   Gregor Maehle, *Mudras: Seals of Yoga* (Crabbes Creek, NSW, Australia: Kaivalya Publications, 2022), 1.

To perform this mudra, follow these steps:

Bring your palms together prayerfully at your heart. Then interlace your pinky and ring fingers so they fold inside your palms. Now you'll extend your middle fingers, making sure the tips touch, and interweave your thumbs and index fingers. These two fingers then form rings around each other, with the fingertips touching. You are now invoking the energies of the earth and bringing them into your first chakra while inviting a grounded state of love.

FIGURE 2: THE MULADHARA MUDRA

SUMMARY

Our first chakra is ultimately an intersection of mind, body, earth, and spirit. Keeping it healthy is essential if we want to better our own everyday lives and accentuate the positive aspects of our shared humanity. We don't need to feel bad about having the fears, stressors, and shadow frequencies associated with the first chakra; they are integral parts of ourselves that allow us to grow. Rather, we can strengthen and balance the root chakra through awareness of its energy and by employing some of the simple practices I have offered here and that you will find throughout this book. Foundational to all your life energies, a healthy first chakra will help you tap into the body's pure magic.

7

SELF-HEALING AND GROUNDING

AMELIA VOGLER

I spent my childhood doing two things that might seem incongruous: roller-skating through my family's funeral home and playing in the abundant nature on the farm where I grew up. Bookended by the teachings of the dead and the birthing and blooming flowers, my early life offered me an educational landscape of the mystical, the natural, and the divine. My compass always pointed toward the big questions in life: *Who am I? What's my purpose? Why is life so short and some lives shorter than others? Where did we come from? Where do we return? Did we ever leave to go beyond or did we bring the beyond with us here?*

Over time, I noticed that all of nature reflects teaching about life, death, and how to live. Ultimately, everything is about the soul, which generates a light within and around every being. Your root chakra plays a foundational role in reflecting this light through your entire physical body. This chakra, often known for its grounding qualities, supports the soul in being (and staying) "home" in your body.

This chapter shares a few deeply grounding self-healing practices that provide simple ways to enhance the relationship between your soul and your body, strengthen the resilience of your root chakra through consistent, simple experiences of embodiment, and ground your soul's core qualities or virtues through the root chakra.

CONNECTING WITH THE EARTH THROUGH PRONE, PRAYERFUL GROUNDING

This practice will help you deeply connect to Mother Earth and enhance the powers of your first chakra. As you perform this practice, you will begin to apply two important lessons in healing for self or others.

First, you must release yourself from outcomes. Setting an intention offers direction to the healing, but this is quite different from defining a specific healing outcome. When you are attached to the outcome, you limit your capacity for healing to only those options you can see. What if greater Spirit has something more significant in store for you? The second lesson in healing is releasing the need to know; basically, it's important to accept *allowing* instead of *knowing*.

When we allow a process, we relax. We release tension, tightness, or diminished energy flow. There is mystery in healing, and getting used to sitting in the space of "not needing to know" will allow energetic space for that mystery to be invited into your healing space.

Preparation

Across almost all major religions, the most reverential type of bowing is accomplished by lying prone, flat on the ground, facedown, arms straight above your head, with your palms down. In this practice, you are not prostrating yourself toward another being or deity but simply lying, honoring your groundedness between soul, body, and earth. In the spiritual sense, the earth is a natural extension of your body, an ancestor of your form.

This practice is also incredibly grounding, as your primary sensory organs are facedown and have restricted stimulus. Your belly is wholly connected to the ground below you. In essence, you are fully open to the ground below you, welcoming that connection as if hugging the ground.

Intention

To establish a sense of grounding in the body to nourish your relationship with the earth.

Steps

» Lie with your belly to the ground. You may turn your head and lay your face to one side for comfort.

» Place your arms to your sides, palms down, or extend yourself fully with your arms over your head and palms to the ground. If mobility is limited, honor your shoulders' range of motion by opening your arms wider.

» Inhale and feel your belly expand into and become one with the earth.

» Exhale and feel the earth extend itself to you. Consider yourself heart to heart and skin to skin with the planet.

» Notice how it feels to connect your whole body to the ground below you. This nourishes and balances your root chakra.

SUPINE FULL-BODY HEALING SCAN

This practice will help you connect to the heavens as well as the earth.

Preparation

When you lie supine (on your back), your spine, the seat of your entire nervous system, is connected to the ground. As you link breath to body, you connect your spiritual awareness to your animal and primal self.

Intention

To bridge your awareness between your energy body and your physical body.

This practice is so simple, but it is the absolute foundation for all other self-healing practices. *You can't change what you can't see, so creating this body-centered awareness is the first step when learning hands-on or self-healing practices.* When you can feel, sense, or experience your energy flowing versus being more sluggish and constricted, you will begin to dialogue between your physical body and your energy body. It is in these conversations that healing is initiated.

Steps

» Lie on your back with your arms at your sides; open your palms down to the earth (or floor) below you.

» Connect with your everyday, regular breath.

» Start at the top of the head and scan your physical and energetic bodies for areas that feel tight or tense or have diminished energy flow. This step involves simply noticing and creating awareness. In some moments this is easier than in others.

» Return to the top of the head and flow from area to area with an intentional breath.

» When you reach an area of tension or one with diminished energetic flow, inhale and send your in-breath to that area. Inspiration means "in spirit," or bringing spirit into the body.

» On the exhale, hold an intention to allow your exhale to release any tension, tightness, or stagnant energy in that area.

» After moving through all the areas that felt tense or constricted, feel, sense, or experience the body as whole and fully integrated. Lie in your wholeness.

» **OPTIONAL.** If there is a color, shape, sound, affirmation, or other root chakra–clearing practice that feels supportive to you, this is the perfect time to offer that practice, as the body's energies are open and flowing and your physical and energetic bodies are in communication.

HANDS-ON ROOT CHAKRA BALANCE

When you are able, it's powerful to use your hands to create first chakra balance for self and others. Following is a deep practice for this.

Preparation

All healing starts in the heart; it is the seat of love, vitality, and essence. The heart also has a protective sheath called the pericardium, which in the meridian system extends to protect the body, mind, and spirit. When you start by holding your heart, you connect both to love—that universal force of healing—and protection. You will offer these energies in service of healing and balancing your root chakra. The love language of the root chakra is safety, and you can extend the pericardium's protective energies to this practice.

Intention

To balance the root chakra with love.

Steps

» Sit in a chair with your feet on the ground.

» Place both hands on your heart and connect your hands to the love that you are.

» While holding your hands on your heart and deepening your connection with love, feel your feet strongly connected to the floor below you.

» Bend down and place one hand on each foot or ankle and offer love to your feet. Hold an intention that love balances the chakras via the feet, perhaps even honoring your walk on the planet. Hold your feet for about a minute.

» Move your hands up to your knees and offer love to them. They represent humility and give you access to profound joy. Hold an intention that love balances your knees. Hold your knees for about a minute.

» Move your hands up to your hips and offer love to them. They help you pivot and change directions in life. Hold an intention that love balances your hips. Hold your hips for about a minute.

» Through intention, visualize energy running from your hips to the ground and moving from the ground to the hips. This will help open all the channels of energy in the legs and support your connection to the earth. Practice sensing the energy movement in your legs.

» Place one hand, palm to your body, between your thighs, about six inches from the base of your perineum. Hold the intention that love balances your root chakra for about a minute.

» Notice what you notice. You may feel an energetic spin, pulling, or pulsing from your root chakra. You may notice that these feelings get more balanced as a bit of time passes.

» Wipe your hands down your legs and tap your feet on the ground to complete the practice. This will help clear any stagnant energy from your legs and root chakra.

CLEARING THE ROOT CHAKRA THROUGH THE INNER WHEEL

Like all chakras, the root chakra has an inner wheel and an outer wheel. Cyndi has been teaching this for a long time. In *Advanced Chakra Healing*, she shares that the inner wheel is encoded by your spirit and regulates your dharmic or spiritual functions, while the outer wheel is programmed by your soul, family issues, and your karma, or issues that must be faced.[9]

The most powerful way to balance our first chakra is to emanate healing from the inner wheel—to spread light throughout, thereby reprogramming any negative ideas in the outer wheel.

Preparation

In this healing practice, you will activate your own light and then the light of various spiritual virtues through the inner wheel of the root chakra.

Intention

To let your own light, the light of the Divine's virtues, provide personal first chakra healing.

The Steps

> » Take a moment and connect to a virtue that you embody in your life. Examples might be integrity, honesty, grace, beauty, ingenuity, creativity, kindness, humor, love, or peace.

---

9   Cyndi Dale, *Advanced Chakra Healing* (Woodbury, MN: Llewellyn Publications, 2021), 348.

» Use your intention and imagine a ball of light filled with this virtue deep in the center of your first chakra hip area.

» Strengthen this ball of light by sending affirmations to honor who you are. This is your inner spirit, located in the inner wheel of your root chakra. Essentially, you are bearing witness to the beauty that you are.

» By intention, allow the energies in this ball to fill, balance, and strengthen your root chakra from the inside. As an example, you might call forth peace and notice how peace becomes you. This illustrates two things: first, you are the vehicle for the virtues, and second, what you call forth from yourself becomes true through the root chakra!

SUMMARY

The root chakra is your foundation, your base, so these practices allow you to come deeper into a connection with the core light of who you are—both connected to yourself and connected to the earth below you. In essence, these practices bring you into an embodied connection with the light that shines in your eyes and further connects you to compassion and honoring the light in all living things.

8

GUIDED MEDITATIONS

AMANDA HUGGINS

As an anxiety coach, yoga teacher, and meditation instructor, I consider meditation an essential practice for anyone who desires more balance in mind, body, and spirit.

There are two things I frequently hear when I recommend meditation to a beginner: "I'm so *bad* at meditating!" and "I know I should be meditating, but it's so hard!" I don't disagree with the latter sentiment; meditation *can* be hard sometimes. As humans we have naturally busy minds, and it can be quite a challenge to sit in stillness for more than a moment or two.

But meditation is not so much a practice of *clearing the mind of all thoughts* as it is *observing and not attaching to the thoughts that come up.* Imagine cloud-gazing on a sunny, carefree day. As you look at the sky, you softly observe the shapes of the clouds: one looks like a butterfly…the next, maybe a sailboat. Cloud after cloud passes as you lazily gaze upward and name the shapes you see. In that scenario, is your mind fully cleared of all thoughts? Of course not! But as the mind softly rests in relaxed observation, you may find you have fewer anxious, ungrounded thoughts. *That* is meditation.

When you distill meditation down to the simple act of *inhaling* and *exhaling*, you're already an expert meditator. When you decided it was time to leave your mother's womb and enter the world, what's the very first thing you did?

You took a big, deep, expansive inhale.

See? You're already a fantastic meditator! You've been doing it since birth.

THE MIND, BODY, AND FIRST CHAKRA CONNECTION

The first chakra and meditation are perfect partners because both are so directly connected to our ability to feel grounded, secure, and stable. A consistent meditation practice has been proven to support the regulation of the central nervous system and the fight-or-flight response. When your fight-or-flight response is activated (often by the anxious mind), it dysregulates your nervous system *and* your energetic system.

From an emotional standpoint, fear is the energy behind fight-or-flight activation; your mind and body have decided you are unsafe, and that sense of fear is transmitted to your first energy center. Not only does the physical body feel ungrounded but the mind and emotions run amok with fear-based stories and negative inner dialogue that perpetuate a narrative of feeling unsafe.

As a Formerly Anxious Person, I lived in an almost constant state of fight-or-flight and experienced long stretches of disconnection from my first chakra. There were a number of things that used to deeply activate my fear, but money was my ultimate first chakra trigger. I spent years living paycheck to paycheck, and just a simple whisper of words like "rent" or "bills" was enough to send me into overdrive. Within seconds, my body would enter a panicked state and my mind would be flooded with fear-based chatter. I was in such a constant state of dysregulation that it was nearly impossible to accept any narrative other than "Money makes me feel unsafe."

Meditation was a key practice in reconnecting with my first chakra and healing that particular fear narrative. I learned to slow down my breathing, stay present to my thoughts, and tune in to my energy center of security. When I began pouring energy and connection into my first chakra, I was finally able to start moving the fear and resistance out of my space.

We all have our unique flavors of fear. For some nothing is more activating than finances. For others it may be romantic relationships or parental trauma. In many cases it's usually not just one thing. I've worked with countless clients who previously expressed that nearly *anything* could trigger their fight-or-flight response.

If you're not yet clear on what (or who) activates your fight-or-flight response, I encourage you to take a few moments to reflect before continuing. Here are four questions to guide your reflection and help you gain clarity on what may be blocking your first chakra:

> » What do I sense blocks or triggers my first chakra the most?
>
> » What creates a sense of insecurity, ungroundedness, or fear in my body? What about in my mind?
>
> » How do these fears manifest in my actions?
>
> » What would my life look like if I were to release myself from these fears?

These questions may offer you another layer of self-understanding and support you in the meditation exercises we'll explore together.

MEDITATION PRACTICES

Before you engage in any of the following first chakra meditations, let's take a moment to review fundamentals.

» **Space.** Because the first chakra is so deeply connected to security, grounding, and safety, I encourage you to create an environment that can mirror those energies back to you. Find your comfiest cushions, your warmest blankets, your coziest socks. Take care in creating or finding a space that will hold and nurture you.

» **Sound.** If sitting in complete silence feels ungrounding, find soothing music to play in the background. For added benefits, you can select music designed specifically for first chakra connection and healing. The 396 Hz frequency is a healing sound that supports the release of fear; a quick internet search will yield hundreds of fantastic recordings to choose from!

» **Body.** If it's available to you, find a cross-legged seat so you can really feel your root chakra connecting with the earth beneath you. You may also choose to lie down and surrender your body weight into the earth—a nice option to reinforce feelings of support and safety.

The following three exercises on visualization, inquiry, and affirmation offer different ways to access your first chakra. You can practice the one you're most called to, blend any of the three practices together, or add on something else you need. Meditation is a free-flowing, deeply personal practice, and I encourage you to use this space to listen and respond to the messages of your first chakra. Remember that *you* hold the keys to your healing.

PRACTICE

HOW TO VISUALIZE

There's no one "right" way to practice visualization in meditation. Some people are quite literally able to "see" shapes, colors, and textures, while others might describe visualization as more of a feeling, a memory, or an inner knowing. However you visualize, trust that what you're doing is right!

Let's begin.

After setting up your space and settling into your body, allow your eyes to close. Use the first three to five cycles of breath (long, slow inhalations and exhalations) to relax into your practice. Notice if stress or anxious thoughts from the day try to take precedence over focusing on the breath. If so, use the exhales to release the distractions and return to your center.

Draw your awareness to the base of the spine and place soft focus on the beautiful red light energy radiating from your first chakra. Breathe.

As you observe this energy center, what subtleties do you notice? What shade or tone of red do you see? How bright is the glow? How far beyond your body does the energy reach?

Let your intuition guide you now as you feel into what you are observing. Perhaps you determine you'd like to turn the "dial" of this energy center's brightness up or down slightly...or you'd like to extend the glow of the chakra...or you'd like it to become a more brilliant shade of red. In your mind's eye, see those adjustments being made until you feel complete.

Stay in the chakra, and take a slow, expansive inhale. As you exhale, see roots growing from your first chakra and reaching deep into the earth below you. Watch as the network of roots spreads easily into the fertile earth beneath you. How far do they reach?

Imagine that the soil your roots are growing in is rich with all the stability, support, and universal healing energy you desire. There is more than enough for you, and you feel that. See your tree roots drink up the safety, stability, and security needed, and cultivate a sense of gratitude. You are supported.

You may feel called to just absorb and receive for a few minutes. Stay with the breath for as long as you'd like.

The lower body may feel especially heavy at times. If it feels comfortable and safe, continue offering your body weight into the ground and enjoy how nice it feels to trust that the earth will support you. You are taken care of.

When you're ready to close your meditation, allow the visuals to fade away and come back to the breath. Take three large inhales to wake the body back up.

PERFORMING INQUIRY

Engaging in meditative self-inquiry is one of my favorite ways to get out of the "logic" brain and into the heart (and, in this case, the root!). When practicing self-inquiry meditation, you focus on a single question or a series of questions (such as "What am I not seeing?" or "What part of me is hiding?") and allow any energetic insights, answers, or healing to move through you.

The following meditation inquiry questions are intended for you to begin dialoguing with your first chakra. In your own inquiry, you may find that other questions arise... which is fantastic! Let your awareness wander to whichever questions you feel will offer you healing and guidance.

Find a comfortable meditation position. Take a few moments to settle into your breath and body, using the fundamentals listed earlier in the chapter. You may also choose to first practice the visualization exercise as a lead-in to your inquiry.

Breathe deeply, and allow all thoughts from the day to simply drain out of your first chakra and into the earth. Stay with this release until the mind is less noisy and the body is more still.

For those with extra-chatty minds, I suggest you visualize turning down the dial of your "logic" brain and turning up the dial on your "heart brain" or "chakra brain" before sitting with inquiry questions.

Place your energy and awareness in your first chakra. Stay there, and choose one or two questions to reflect upon. Below are some of my favorite first chakra inquiries:

» What does safety feel like to me?

» Where do I experience safety in my body?

» What blocks are sitting in my first chakra?

» What does my chakra want me to hear, feel, or know?

» How can I create more grounding in my life?

You may want to keep a journal nearby to jot down any insights that come forward. Breathe and receive, continuing to surrender into the ever-unfolding conversation with your first chakra.

When you feel complete, thank your body, your energy system, and your heart for participating. Take a few gentle breaths to bring yourself back into your body.

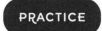

PRACTICE

EMPLOYING AFFIRMATION

You can use this meditation practice to begin affirming how you want to feel. It's a lovely, gentle way to shift your inner dialogue and champion positive belief systems. Through a regular "I am" affirmation practice, you will take ownership of your energy, narratives, and negatively patterned thinking.

"I am" affirmations are a choose-your-own-adventure type of meditation; you can alter your mantra in response to how you (and your first chakra) are feeling. Perhaps one day you're feeling disconnected, so you might choose a mantra like "I am grounded" to inspire thoughts and feelings of security. Another day you may be feeling wonderfully grounded and use the same mantra to celebrate the fantastic feelings you're already experiencing.

Below are some sample mantras and suggestions for when to use them.

- » "I am safe" for days when you're experiencing fear.

- » "I am home" to create or reinforce security and groundedness in your body.

- » "I am taken care of" or "I am protected" when you are feeling unsupported or distracted by your external environment.

- » "I am rooted" or "I am stable" when you're feeling especially unstable.

- » "I am connected" to strengthen the bond between you, your energy centers, and all that exists beyond you.

- » Simply chant "I am" to affirm your energy.

- » Chant the first chakra seed sound, *Lam* ("lum"). This is a wonderful option at any time, but especially during days when words escape you.

Take a moment to tune into your energy. As you begin to breathe deeply, feel into which mantra your soul is craving.

On your inhales, repeat "I am" as you draw energy into the first chakra.

On your exhales, repeat the word or words of your choosing as you exhale and take root into the earth beneath you. Continue.

Allow yourself to get lost in the cyclical nature of the breath as you repeat your mantra. Invite the feelings or qualities associated with your "I am" mantra into your body. Remain in your breath for at least five minutes…but you might find you want to stay much longer!

When you feel ready to close out your meditation, take one large inhale and reach your arms up and out overhead. Feel your spine extend from root to crown as you stretch upward and softly pause for a moment with the lungs full. As you exhale and bring your hands to heart center, offer up one final prayer to yourself, your guides, and the universe: "Thank you."

SUMMARY

The beautiful thing about meditation is that it's a completely free, no-frills tool that yields high returns. It's more about observing your thoughts without judgment than monitoring them closely. You can also pledge that every time you deeply exhale, you take a step toward regulating your nervous system by releasing fear, and that every time you inhale, you're welcoming in fresh air and energy to replace the fear you just released.

9

VIBRATIONAL REMEDIES

JO-ANNE BROWN

My journey in energy medicine began in my early thirties, when I experienced significant health problems as a result of first chakra imbalances. My enthusiasm for life vanished, and I found it difficult to study, work, or be present in my relationships. I had no energy, and I felt unsafe. Daily panic attacks, regular migraine headaches, and chronic digestive issues plagued me. After much searching, I found a local practitioner specializing in a frequency-based modality who worked with me to restore my first chakra energies.

Like many energy healers, I started my own energy medicine practice after my transformative healing. I cannot imagine doing this work without vibrational remedies; they are an essential part of my energetic tool kit. Over the last twenty-five years, I have witnessed many miraculous energetic shifts by applying vibrational remedies that support the first chakra.

We know that the first chakra represents physical energy. But the first chakra is so much more than just physicality! Remember, more than 99.999 percent of an object's energy is subtle energy. When we view the first chakra as purely physical, we miss out on the rich depth of subtle energies contained within it, including the archetypical energy of the Mother, the attribute of patience, kundalini activity, affection, loving touch, and the qualities of security, safety, and abundance.

Here, I will increase your awareness of how vibrational remedies support and empower the first chakra by

> » describing what they are

> » explaining how they benefit us

> » exploring the difference between support-based and tangible remedies

> » listing several first chakra remedies

> » providing two practices to support you at home

WHAT ARE VIBRATIONAL REMEDIES?

Vibrational energies help alter disharmonic energies in order to return us to a state of flow or balance. We know that our first chakra has physical duties. It also has psychological and spiritual functions. These include our thoughts and belief systems, emotions, imprints (or genetic patterning), family history, ancestral lineage, and backgrounds. Vibrational remedies can be true agents of support for our first chakra, mainly working within the guidelines of resonance.

WHAT IS RESONANCE?

Our energetic response to vibrational remedies is known as resonance. Resonance occurs when one object is vibrating at the same natural frequency as a second object and forces the second object into vibrational motion.

In the world of music, the outcome of resonance is sound. In the world of vibrational healing, resonance occurs when a person energetically experiences the beneficial effects of a vibrational remedy. Sometimes these remedies benefit us by energetically reminding us of our first chakra strengths. At other times they inform, educate, and attune us to the changes we need to make in order to reflect more positive first chakra attributes.

Ultimately, the human experience exposes us to energies (physical, psychological, and spiritual) that are either resonant or dissonant. Our personal first chakra energies naturally resonate with healthy first chakra energies and are in dissonance with energies that are harmful or degenerative to our first chakra. It is that simple!

THE BIOPHYSICAL MODEL OF MEDICINE

Vibrational remedies are based on the biophysical model of medicine rather than on the mechanistic model of conventional Western medicine. The biophysical model recognizes that energetic (biophysical) signals occur within our bodies before physical changes in our cell chemistry do.

The biophysical model is based on the premise that biophysical signals are delivered electromagnetically through frequencies, or vibrational information. After all, as living organisms, we are fields of energy; we are electrical beings. Each healthy living cell in our body produces a membrane potential: a small measurable electrical charge of around seventy millivolts. When the membrane potential drops, our cells start to become unhealthy. And when our cells no longer have a measurable membrane potential, they are no longer living cells.

Biophysicists believe that illness results from disrupted cell communication, which leads to the failure of our autoregulation systems. When we introduce healthy energetic signals into the body, the communication between cells is improved and the body's natural healing capacity is supported.

This communication is crucial during the active development of the first chakra in a new living human being. Just after conception, multiple cell divisions are taking place at a rapid rate, and the first chakra is already converting subtle energies, in the form of vibrational signals, into physical form. As this happens, countless unseen but highly influential factors are being embodied, including familial programming that shapes values and belief systems.

VIBRATIONAL REMEDIES FOR OUR FIRST CHAKRA

Vibrational remedies fall into one of two categories:

» support-based remedies
» tangible remedies

Support-Based Vibrational Remedies

Support-based vibrational remedies include treatments, therapies, and practices that work with subtle energies. They generally require the presence and guidance of a healing practitioner, and they support our first chakra energies through one of these methods:

» skin-to-skin contact (such as acupressure, acupuncture, kinesiology, massage, reflexology, and therapeutic touch techniques)

» vibrational media (such as color/crystal/chakra therapies, frequency-based modalities, sound/vocal therapy, Reiki, and toning)

» demonstrational guidance (such as yoga and Emotional Freedom Technique [EFT] tapping)

I'm next going to examine three of the modalities just described. First, I'll feature two methods that relate to the vibrational media: sound therapies and frequency-based modalities. Second, I'll explore EFT, which fits into the demonstrational guidance category. I'll leave you to adventure into skin-to-skin contact because these processes are so effective when a practitioner is administering them. Of course, there are many techniques for self-healing too, which you can journey into other books and on the internet to discover. I've selected the three subjects I've shared because they are potent and it's easy to find ways to perform healing with them on yourself as well as via a practitioner.

SOUND THERAPIES: Some of the purest vibrational remedies are sound-based therapies that use music and sound to energetically support the first chakra. Various instruments and tools can be used in this process, including musical instruments (drums and cymbals), crystal singing bowls, tuning forks, and rain sticks.

In my healing work, I use the solfeggio frequencies that align with the physical plane (from numerology) to support the first chakra (174, 417, and 741 Hz). My favorite is the 174 Hz frequency, which is particularly beneficial for those suffering from extreme pain and trauma.

Other frequencies that provide significant vibrational support for the first chakra are 432 and 228 Hz.

FREQUENCY-BASED THERAPIES: These therapies use low-voltage frequency–generating devices (such as the Rife machine) to send therapeutic vibrations to the body through conductive electrodes.

During a therapy session, these vibrations are received by the human body at the cellular level and improve cell communication by supporting cells that have reduced membrane potentials.

Frequency-based therapies allow us to move "stuck" first chakra energies using specific customized frequencies to activate blocked kidney and bladder meridian channels and support the organ systems managed by the first chakra. These include the adrenal glands, the urinary system, the coccygeal vertebrae, and eliminatory organs.

EFT TAPPING: EFT tapping is a vibrational practice for addressing physical pain or emotional distress. It involves a systematic process of tapping on specific meridian points with our fingertips as we speak targeted phrases.

Tapping is inherently supportive of our first chakra because it directly addresses the fundamental first chakra issues of safety, security, and abundance. This practice provides vibrational support for many people who suffer from severe first chakra conditions, including trauma, PTSD, anxiety, depression, fears, and phobias.

EFT tapping activates the bladder and kidney meridians (both managed by the first chakra), so it is a vibrational remedy that is ideally suited to first chakra problems.

Tangible Vibrational Remedies

Unlike support-based remedies, tangible vibrational remedies are literal "medicines." They can be received into the body orally (via drops and small pills), through the skin (using oils, ointments, and salves), or via diffusion methods (such as essential oils).

These vibrational remedies include homeopathic remedies, flower essences, and essential oils. They also include infused objects that intrinsically support us through their presence in our environment—including crystals, jewelry, amulets, and other material objects.

HOMEOPATHIC REMEDIES: Homeopathy is a system of alternative medicine developed by Samuel

Hahnemann in the late eighteenth century based on the premise that "like cures like": that a substance that produces symptoms of an illness in a healthy person can, in significantly smaller doses, treat an illness with similar symptoms.

Different homeopathic potencies (low, medium, high, and very high) target different energetic levels within the body, including physical, mental, emotional, psychological, and constitutional.

During diagnosis, a homeopathic practitioner will use the principle of resonance to ensure an appropriate customized remedy is prescribed to facilitate healing.

Homeopathic remedies that support our first chakra include Aconite, Arnica, Cocculus, Gelsemium, and Pulsatilla. When conditions have physically manifested in the body, the lower-potency remedies are most suitable to promote physical healing.

FLOWER ESSENCES: Plant remedies have been widely used by many cultures since the early 1500s, when Swiss physician and alchemist Paracelsus collected dew from flowers to treat his patients' emotional imbalances.

Ancient herbalists frequently apply the doctrine of signatures concept to determine the healing properties of plants. This is another principle of resonance that means certain distinguishing features of the plant (such as shape, color, or scent) indicate its healing properties. For example, red plants and flowers are supportive of blood and our bodily organs that process blood.

This concept was used in the creation of many types of flower essence remedies. I'm featuring Bach flower and Australian bushflower essences because I've experienced their power for myself and with clients.

» *Bach flower remedies:* In the early 1900s, Edward Bach formulated thirty-eight liquid flower-based remedies and his famous customized blend, Rescue Remedy, as a system to support people as they work through specific emotions and come into emotional and holistic balance. Bach flower remedies that support our first chakra include Rescue Remedy for stress relief, Aspen (for security), Rock Rose (for courage), Impatiens (for patience), and Mimulus (for facing fears).

» *Australian bushflower essences:* Australian Ian White is a fifth-generation herbalist who learned at a young age that Aborigines often resolved their emotional imbalances by eating flowers they found in the bush. He formulated sixty-nine individual liquid flower-based remedies and twelve customized blends to balance and harmonize our well-being by supporting our subtle energies. Australian bushflower remedies that support the first chakra include Emergency Essence (for comfort, reassurance, and courage), Abund Essence (for poverty consciousness,) Dynamis Essence (for restoring vital energy,) Dog Rose (for fears and insecurities), and Macrocarpa (for restoring endurance and enthusiasm).

Following are two vibrational practices you can use to support your first chakra.

OPEN TO ABUNDANCE USING A SIMPLIFIED VERSION OF EFT

Do you want to attract abundance and prosperity into your life? This simple practice activates four aspects of your first chakra so you can easily receive material provisions.

» Find a comfortable space where you will not be disturbed. Sit facing north.

» Tap on both your collarbones (this is kidney meridian point KI-27) with the index and middle fingers of both hands. As you do this, speak the words "I activate positive first chakra vibrations that allow me to easily receive abundance and material provisions."

» Continue to tap and repeat this statement a total of eight times.

» Hold both hands upward toward the sky and visualize that you are receiving all your material needs, wants, and more.

» Repeat this practice daily.

PRACTICE

CREATE AN ARTWORK REMEDY INFUSED WITH PROTECTION

Would you like to create a remedy infused with protective, safe energies? Then this is the practice for you! You will need a square painting canvas; black, red, and yellow acrylic paint; a one-inch paintbrush; and a small handful of sand. These three colors are used in numerous cultures because of the meaning they invoke. For instance, on the Lakota medicine wheel, yellow represents the sun, black speaks to the day's end, red references active power, and white (which is most likely the color of the canvas) is related to warmth. As well, these three colors show up in the first chakra—black equal to soil for grounding, red the typical coloration of that chakra, and yellow the hue of the earth element. We'll further clarify coloration in chapter 12.

» Before you start to paint, set the intention that the artwork you are creating will be infused with the energy of protection and safety for yourself or for the person receiving it.

» Paint your canvas (including the edges) with the black acrylic paint and allow it to dry.

» Using the yellow paint, draw your chosen symbol of protection in the center of the canvas. It could be the yellow square at the center of the first chakra yantra described on page 21 or any other symbol of your choosing.

» Outline your chosen symbol of protection with red paint.

» While the paint is still wet, sprinkle sand lightly on your painting and allow it to dry.

» Hang your infused remedy above your bed or in a room where you spend a lot of time.

This practice can also be done on behalf of babies while their first chakras are developing (in utero up to six months of age).

SUMMARY

The purpose of vibrational remedies is to move, unblock, or balance our first chakra life energy. When this occurs, we are strengthened and empowered at the most foundational level of our energetic systems.

Everything, seen and unseen, holds a vibration. Our first chakra subtle energies extend far beyond just the physical realm. When we understand this, we recognize there is a truly limitless range of healing options available to us to support our first chakra!

I encourage you to play with vibrational remedies that support your first chakra. Start with the two practices I just shared and then explore some of the other remedies in this chapter, being guided by your intuition. May you have as much fun with them as I do!

10

CRYSTALS, MINERALS, AND STONES

MARGARET ANN LEMBO

Vim and vigor, focus and strength, abundance and prosperity: these sum up the key energies of the root chakra. The first chakra grounds your spirit into this earthly body. That's one of the reasons I enjoy using crystals, minerals, and stones for chakra balance and alignment. These precious gifts of the earth bring sparkle, shine, and vibrant color to your spiritual journey.

The root chakra is the foundation on which all the other chakras are built. Connecting you with Mother Earth, gemstones are allies and tools for your time here on this planet.

THE POWER OF INTENTION

As Cyndi informed you in the beginning of part 2, intention is all-powerful. It is crucial for activating the subtle capabilities of gemstones. And when a gemstone is paired with a daily affirmation, the stone amplifies and helps you maintain your focus on that intention.

It's easy to choose the perfect stone to match your intention. Simply focus on the image or thought of your intention, then look at the choices of crystals available to you—either in a store or in your own private collection. I'll provide my recommendations on which stones to use, but trust your own inner guidance. If you are attracted to a stone, go with your gut. Match your positive thought with that gemstone and watch your world realign with what you decided you want to create.

PROSPERITY

Prosperity consciousness resides in the root chakra and incorporates all the belief systems you have about money. How do you feel about being wealthy? Do you like rich people? Do you feel you deserve to be paid for your work? How did your family deal with money? Do you save money? Can you accept that there is plenty for everyone and everyone can be prosperous? These foundational beliefs are formed at a very young age.

Abundance and financial security are available to everyone. Here are my go-to prosperity favorites:

Citrine has been known as the "merchant's stone" and pairs well with green aventurine (see below) to draw in the money and abundance you desire. Citrine helps bring clarity and confidence. It takes courage to make things happen the way you want them to, and citrine delivers a vibration that is sure to uplift and improve self-esteem. Use an affirmation like this one: *I am confident and courageous. I shine my light brightly. Prosperity abounds in my life. Goodness multiplies. Whatever I desire, imagine, and passionately act upon becomes reality.*

Emerald is the green variety of the mineral beryl. Emerald is a stone of abundance and extreme wealth. Use this precious gem to focus on well-being and all that is good. With your health and vitality intact, use this stone to attract financial success through your focused actions. Trust that you can be successful and prosperous in a loving and healthy way. Simply activate your inner entrepreneur through focused study. Use your acquired knowledge to reach your goals. These are good thoughts to state with emerald in your presence: *I am successful in all my pursuits. My actions have beneficial results for everyone. I have excellent business skills. I earn unlimited income doing what I love.*

Green aventurine helps you stay focused on eating well and exercising regularly to maintain a healthy heart. On another level, this is a prosperity stone. Keep one in your wallet, pocket, or cash drawer to continue to attract the physical rewards that come with financial success. It's almost as if you have a four-leaf clover in your pocket! Simply recognize your good fortune. Focus on your vast abundance, and you will attract more. Believe that all your travel flows with ease and providence. Use these thoughts repetitively with some green aventurine on hand: *I am so incredibly lucky! I have many blessings in my life. Abundance and prosperity are constantly flowing in my life.*

Jade is a name for two minerals with similar toughness and appearance. Jadeite is the more highly prized, harder mineral, while nephrite is more prolific and is softer. Jade is historically associated with good luck and beneficial results. This royal gem dates back to 3000 BCE and was used in the ancient Chinese culture as a symbol of wealth and high ranking. Jade reminds you to think positively and stay focused on good outcomes. It is also helpful for visualizing ideas and beneficial results. Think these good thoughts with jade in hand: *I am healthy, happy, and prosperous. I am extremely lucky.*

VITAL ENERGY

The energy vibrating at the root chakra, or lack thereof, regulates your health and your passion for life. Do you have a lot of get-up-and-go or are you always tired? You may need more rest or better nutrition to restore your vital life force. Are you a mover and shaker or are you a procrastinator? If you find that you can't conjure up the energy to get things done, it's time to light a fire under your root chakra and get things moving. Your lack of motivation, laziness, or procrastination could stem from depression or inadequate nutrition. Red stones are the way to go when you need more vital energy. Here are a few to help you along the way:

Garnet is a stone to activate passion for life. Garnet keeps you focused on your creative power. Carrying the vibration of passion and determination, this red gem helps you follow through on your goals. Use it when you need to stop procrastinating and get motivated. Garnet is a good stone to work with when you are in the process of manifesting. It helps you take charge of a situation and make things happen. I like these affirmations when I want to get things done: *I have plenty of energy and plenty to share. I am vital and strong! I live a full, passionate life. I am determined.*

Red jasper helps you put an end to procrastination. Use this stone when you have a task at hand that requires focus and mental endurance for successful completion. It is the stone of diligence. Use it to maintain steadfast action to achieve any goal. Red jasper reactivates your passion for living when you've been feeling apathetic, unemotional, or spiritually defunct. This stone is useful for restoring, regenerating, and rejuvenating your passion and libido. A stone of fertility, it supports a healthy pregnancy and birth. With a bit of red jasper, think or say these good thoughts: *I am grounded and focused on the task at hand. I complete projects. I am motivated to accomplish all that needs to be done.*

Red goldstone is a human-made glass containing crystallized copper. The fact that it is a human-made stone doesn't make it any less valuable. Goldstone helps you stay focused on happy thoughts. It is a feel-good stone that carries the good vibrations of well-being and joy. When used with conscious intention, this stone can increase your self-confidence and self-esteem. The brilliant sparkles within the stone help remind you of your magnificence and encourage you to shine your light brightly and with confidence. Affirm and state: *I am abundant. I'm an amazing manifester! I have plenty of energy to get everything done. I have what I need.*

Ruby is the red variety (orangish-red to purplish-red) of the mineral corundum, which is aluminum oxide. Ruby increases your passion for life when used with conscious intent. This brilliant gemstone is a motivational tool to help you complete tasks. Wear a ruby in jewelry or carry one with you if you've been procrastinating. Use it to get your mind wrapped around the idea that it is time to move forward and act. If you want a bit more pizzazz in your life, get a ruby and say: *Vital life force flows vibrantly through me. I am strong and healthy. I'm self-motivated to be productive.*

FOCUS

If you notice that you are a bit spacey and scattered in your thoughts and actions and just can't focus, visualize roots growing from the soles of your feet into the earth, grounding you. Imagine that you are pulling the earth's consciousness through your whole being. Being grounded, focused, and prosperous is the result of a balanced root chakra. Imagine that you are reconnecting with the earth while holding brown or black stones with the clear intention to maintain focus and concentration. Set a strong intention as you incorporate these gems into your life:

Andalusite, also known as chiastolite, has a black cross in its center. Andalusite helps you align with earth-centered spirituality. The grounding elements of andalusite aid in maintaining focus. It is especially useful when you find that staying targeted on the task at hand is challenging. It is a stone for those who jump from one great idea to another but can't seem to complete anything. Gaze at the cross running through the stone to find focus, then think these thoughts: *I am grounded. Protective energies keep me safe always.*

Brown agate is a perfect stone for connecting with the elemental spirits, natural forces, and the fairy kingdom: in other words, Mother Earth. Plant and other earth spirits are aligned with this stone. It is easy to get distracted, go off on tangents, and never get anything done, but this stone can gently keep you on task while still allowing the energy of fun, play, and creativity. Use the negative ions of nature and have some brown agate on hand while you state positive thoughts like these: *I am a caretaker of the earth. I spend time in nature. I am aligned, focused, and grounded.*

Galena is a lead sulfide that helps you stay focused and on task so you can more easily integrate material into your consciousness, making it readily available when you need to retrieve it. It helps you find the foundation you need to stabilize your life, whatever that means to you. Make it your intention to see the silver lining and use these good thoughts: *I'm grounded, focused, and tuned in to the universe. I stay on task with the projects at hand. Challenging situations are transformed and the good is revealed.*

Smoky quartz helps eliminate doubt and worry when you are faced with chaos and confusion. This stone helps you feel safe and sound. With your focused intent, smoky quartz helps amplify your feelings of security. It is also an excellent tool for realigning scattered energy and releasing emotionally charged thoughts and feelings. Believe yourself when you repeat these affirmations: *I am divinely protected. I easily refocus my efforts away from distractions. I honor my grounded connection with Mother Earth.*

PROTECTION

Safety is another aspect of being strongly rooted. Keeping negative energy away is a logical way to maintain safety. Feeling safe and protected is a state of mind. Decide that you are safe and also make smart decisions with your life. Within the kingdom of gemstones, the all-time favorite stones for deflecting negativity and promoting feelings of safety are the black stones and the metallic ones like the following:

Black obsidian is a grounding stone. It is beneficial for maintaining a positive outlook by keeping negative thoughts at bay. This volcanic black glass reminds you that you can turn to others for support while you allow your feelings of grief to take their normal course, which can be very rocky at times. Grounding yourself is important to accomplish your goals. Use these affirmations: *I am focused. I am responsible. I stay with matters until they reach completion. I accomplish whatever I set out to do. I pay attention to what is going on around me.*

Black tourmaline helps clear away repetitive, outdated thoughts so you can achieve your goals. Use it to shield yourself from the effects of jealousy. It also facilitates order in the face of general chaos. Focus your intention on deflecting negativity and surround yourself in a loving cloak of protection while you affirm the following: *I am safe and* *sound. I am always divinely protected. I am enveloped in a sphere of goodness and well-being. I surround myself with trustworthy people.*

Hematite enhances meditation practice. It is well known to promote relaxation for the body, mind, and soul. Hematite removes scattered energy from your energy field and repels negative thoughts. Use hematite to transform a negative situation in your life. With hematite in hand, feel your roots taking hold in the earth and think these good thoughts: *I am calm and peaceful. My roots absorb goodness from the all-giving, bountiful earth, which fills me up and brings me serenity.*

Pyrite helps strengthen courage and self-confidence. Use this stone when you need the guts to set boundaries and stand up for yourself. It helps you feel empowered. Pyrite is a stone of financial abundance. Use this stone with intention when you are trying to improve your financial status. Realign your beliefs by repeating the following thoughts: *I am prosperous and abundant in all facets of my life. I enjoy the many favorable opportunities that are presented to me.*

SELECT A STONE FOR
AN EXACT FIRST CHAKRA NEED

Picking a stone for a first chakra reason is a fantastic way to support a goal. This short exercise will help you tap into your intuition to select a stone and then decide how to best use it for support.

Grab a paper and pen and settle into a quiet place. Then take notes as you reflect on these steps.

» I would like to use a stone to assist me with this focus: _____

» I'd qualify my use of this stone as meeting one of the following needs:
  • prosperity
  • vital energy
  • focus
  • protection

» Review the stones described under the category that you choose. Select one of them and figure out how you're going to obtain that stone. Once you have, then complete this exercise with the next two steps.

» My affirmation for this stone is as follows:

_____

_____

» I am going to employ the stone in a particular
  way. Choices include the following:
  - carrying it around (also decide how)
  - putting it on an altar or other sacred site
  - meditating with it (also determine how
    often and in what way)
  - using it as jewelry
  - sleeping near it
  - other: _____

You can apply this exercise in any way you desire, embrac-
ing different focuses and various stones.

SUMMARY

Crystals, minerals, and stones are terrific tools for healing
first chakra issues. They offer protection, free up vital energy, and provide focus to help you achieve your highest
potential.

11

MANTRA HEALING

Mantras have the power to transform your life. Do you know that adage "Change your thinking and you'll change your life"? That was true for me. Until my daughter was born, I spent my life without much direction or clarity; it felt like life just kind of happened to me. I definitely wasn't living from a place of empowerment. I was at the mercy of my incessantly chattering mind, which was mostly operating on a negative thought loop. And for much of my early adulthood, I struggled with classic root chakra issues: financial insecurity, feelings of unworthiness, poor relationship choices, and more.

My daughter's arrival shone a bright light on what wasn't working in my life, and I became driven to heal my childhood wounds and make the changes necessary to be the best version of myself I could be. One of the most impactful tools in my transformation was mantra healing. With consistent practice, it helped me bring my chattering mind to heel, changed my thinking, and ultimately changed my life. Mantras can help you too.

In this chapter we will explore what mantras are, why they work, and how to create powerful mantras you can use to focus your mind, change your thinking, balance your root chakra, and enhance your overall happiness and well-being.

WHAT IS A MANTRA?

The word *mantra* derives from Vedic Sanskrit and is described as a sacred word, sound, or phrase: a sacred utterance. *Man* means mind or to think and *tra* means tool, so a mantra is literally a tool used to guide and focus the mind.

There are different schools of thought on using traditional mantras versus personal mantras, also known as affirmations. Some believe that affirmations do not contain benefits and that only ancient sacred Sanskrit phrases are true mantras as they contain special vibrational frequencies as well as the energy and intentions of the millions of people who have recited them over millennia. But I know from my own experience, and from the work I do with clients, that there is great power in creating personal mantras that are targeted to a specific feeling and outcome.

So in this chapter, in addition to covering traditional Sanskrit mantras, we will explore how to create powerful personal mantras designed to bring about meaningful transformation. As to which to choose (and you can try both), there are as many options for choosing a mantra as there are people; you get to decide what feels right for you based on the outcome you intend. Whatever your choice, repetition is the key.

MANTRAS AND THE POWER OF THOUGHTS

The human mind is a thinking machine. We have thousands of random thoughts a day, thoughts with no intentional focus or guidance, and interestingly, when we slow down to notice them, we often find that most of those thoughts are negative. We may be worrying about the future, regretting something from the past, or beating ourselves up over this or that. We're all familiar with that little voice in our head that tells us we're not good enough, don't know enough, aren't *whatever* enough. The good news is there's a way to silence that voice and focus the mind in the direction of our choosing, and in doing so transform our lives in whatever way we desire.

Your thought patterns are formed by your life experiences and influenced by your family of origin, peers, culture, and the society in which you live. Every thought you think strengthens the "circuitry" in your brain known as neural pathways, either reinforcing an existing neural pathway or creating a new one. Think of neural pathways as grooves in a dirt road you're driving on: when you're running in those grooves, it's hard to get the tires out—but once you do, you can begin to form new grooves and travel a new path, and eventually the old, unused path will disappear.

Modern brain science has proven that our brains are malleable, that they have neural plasticity, and that we have the ability to rewire our brains at any age. We can use mantras to form new grooves, and with repetition, the old, formerly dominant neural pathways diminish. This physical change in our brain improves our overall well-being, boosts our mood and energy level, eases anxiety, and even strengthens our memory.

PRACTICE

CREATE A MANTRA, STEP 1: THE RANDOM THOUGHT LOG

Before deciding which mantra is best for balancing your root chakra, it's helpful to understand your thought patterns. I recommend taking a few days to become familiar with them by using what I call a random thought log (RTL), a simple and effective tool I created and use both for myself and for my clients.

Set the intention right now to pause throughout the day, take notice of what you were just thinking, and make a note of it in your phone's note app or in a notebook or journal. This will be your RTL. Try setting the timer on your phone for one hour. When it goes off:

> » jot down what you were just thinking
>
> » reset the timer for an hour

It's just that simple. Repeat these steps three or four times a day for two to four days.

This shouldn't take you more than thirty seconds or so. As you track your random thoughts, you will begin to see patterns in your habitual thinking. After a few days, review your notes and discern any patterns you see that relate to the first chakra. Do you find yourself worrying about the future—and whether you'll be safe? Do you continually tell yourself that you'll never have the energy to take the actions needed to improve your life? Whatever emerges, don't criticize yourself for these thoughts; for now you are just looking at patterns.

CREATE A MANTRA, STEP 2:
SHIFT A THOUGHT PATTERN

The next step is to choose whichever thought pattern you wish to change and create a mantra to transform it. First, write down the negative thought pattern you identified. Then write down a brief present-tense positive statement to counter that thought.

For example, I sometimes struggle with charging appropriately for the work I do. My random thoughts may go something like this: *Maybe they wouldn't want to pay that much, but I should have charged my stated price. Why did I feel compelled to give such a discount?* My thinking mind knows my value, but there's still a part of me that doesn't believe I'm worth it (this, by the way, is a common subconscious belief among women). Here are two mantras I've created to counter this negative belief:

> » I love doing my work and am richly rewarded creatively and financially.

> » I am successful doing what I love.

Use this example to do your own two-step process of creating an affirmative personal mantra. Keep it simple and repeat it consistently throughout the day, especially when you notice your mind wandering toward that habitual negative thought pattern.

WORKING WITH A
TRADITIONAL SANSKRIT MANTRA

The longevity of this practice speaks to its enduring impact. Traditionally, *Lam* (pronounced "lum") is the mantra for the root chakra. It is a *bija* (seed) mantra, and its frequency is that of an optimally healthy root chakra. When this energy center becomes unbalanced, it can cause a lot of anxiety. Through the law of entrainment, when we chant *Lam*, we bring the root chakra back into homeostasis, diminishing the anxiety that results from unbalanced root chakra emotions. This mantra is best practiced aloud, thinking *Lam* as you inhale through the nose and speaking *Lam* as you exhale. This is also a perfect mantra for japa meditation, which I will discuss below.

Another powerful Sanskrit mantra is *Om Namah Shivaya*. It means "I bow to Shiva, or the inner self." It's said that chanting this mantra is a pathway to knowing and understanding your innermost self. Chanting *Om Namah Shivaya* while meditating can create a powerful feeling of belonging and well-being, countering first chakra feelings of unworthiness and lack of safety. When we come to truly know ourselves, we can understand our cosmic nature and our connection to all that is and fully know that we belong.

MORE PRACTICES FOR ENJOYING MANTRAS

There are many other ways to use mantras: meditation, chanting, and journaling, to name a few. I'll describe a few more you can mix into your earth-star approaches.

Meditation

Meditation is a powerful practice that, according to numerous studies, can literally transform the brain. If you already have a meditation practice, you can incorporate a mantra into your practice by repeating it silently in your mind or softly repeating it aloud. If you don't currently have a meditation practice, why not give it a try now? Many people believe you have to sit for long periods of time to receive the benefits of meditation, but the truth is that you can start with as little as three minutes, and incorporating a mantra will help focus your mind.

Find a comfortable seated position on the floor or on a sofa or chair. Sit with your back straight. Set a timer if you like. Take a few deep breaths, inhaling through your nose and exhaling through your mouth, to relax yourself and become fully present. Close your eyes or if you prefer leave them slightly open with a soft focus. Let your breathing resume its normal rhythm and begin repeating your mantra, either silently or softly aloud. When your mind wanders—and it will—this is not a problem; simply come back to your mantra.

When you're through, take notice of how you're feeling. If you can cultivate the habit of meditating daily with your mantra as the focus of your attention, you are sure to notice the benefits.

Chanting

Chanting is another method to use with your mantra. Japa meditation—meditating with the aid of a necklace called a mala consisting of 108 beads (also called prayer beads)—is a beautiful way to chant a mantra. There is a wide range of available mala materials and price ranges to choose from; find one that speaks to you. You can use any mantra you like, but I recommend beginning this practice with *Lam*, the bija mantra for the root chakra.

For japa meditation, take a comfortable seated position and hold your mala in your right hand between thumb and index finger, with your middle, ring, and pinkie fingers together. Notice that one bead is different from the others in shape or may have a tassel—that's the "guru bead," and it marks the starting and ending point of the 108 beads. Drape your mala over your middle finger with your thumb on the guru bead. Use your thumb to lightly pull one bead at a time toward you as you chant your mantra, repeating the mantra with each bead.

There are several benefits to using a mala in your meditations and rituals:

» It increases focus as it is an efficient and practical tool for counting mantras and is an easy way to keep track of how many times you have recited it.

» Physical contact with prayer beads transmits their inherent healing powers.

» Once the mala is infused with the intention of your mantra, you can use it as a touchstone throughout your day to keep your mantra in your consciousness.

Kirtan

A magical way to experience mantras is through *kirtan*, a traditional practice consisting of the call-and-response chanting of Sanskrit mantras. Usually it qualifies as more of a group practice than one you conduct solo.

It's typically done in a group setting with one person chanting or singing the mantra and the group chanting or singing it in response. In this practice, only traditional Sanskrit mantras are used. Many yoga studios offer kirtan practices, but you can also find kirtan online to practice in the privacy of your home. It is uplifting and definitely worth exploring if you want to infuse your first chakra (and all your chakras) with a sense of well-being.

Journaling

Journaling is another way to work with your mantra as a kind of written meditation. In your journal or a notebook, simply write out the mantra you created in the two-part practice earlier in this chapter. Write it over and over again as you also think it in your mind. You can do this for a set amount of time or for however long feels good to you. When you've finished, you may want to do a few minutes of stream-of-consciousness journaling, writing down whatever comes to mind without giving it any thought. This can be a very informative practice that, if done over a period of time, may reveal and heal hidden subconscious beliefs originating in your first chakra.

SUMMARY

Incorporating mantras into your daily life can reap huge rewards, including increased self-awareness, reduced stress, a greater sense of ease and well-being, increased self-compassion, and a more positive outlook in general—terrific healing for the first chakra. Make the practice your own by trying a number of the methods in this chapter to discover which ones feel right for you. Whatever you decide, I have no doubt you will find that cultivating a mantra practice is transformative.

12

COLORS AND SHAPES

GINA NICOLE

Among the many fabulous ways to activate and attune your first chakra and naturally expand into optimal living, two of my favorites are using shapes and drawing on a full spectrum of colors. This chapter will provide inspiration for you to explore these powerful energy healing techniques on your own to support a strong, balanced first chakra.

As a practitioner of subtle energy medicine, my passion is empowering people like you to realize their full potential by taking control of their subtle energy and embodying who they were born to be. My journey began with feng shui, using the art of placement in my home and office to move energy. That was when I began to learn how shape and color helped transmute the energy around me.

In my mid-twenties, I had a rock-bottom moment when my body was in so much pain that it kept me up for hours at night. I was inflamed with anger and carrying extra weight, and to be blunt, nothing was flowing properly, including my bowels.

No matter what I tried—doctors, medications, the healing arts—nothing gave me that boost of energy I craved. While I couldn't pinpoint the source at the time, my first chakra was a spinning wheel digging deep into the mud, and I was desperate to find a solution.

I started making changes to my home that went beyond feng shui, manipulating colors and shapes in my environment in other ways. My healing began to unfold in a new way. My body released weight, I felt energized again, my digestive system got back on track, and my dating life opened up after a heartbreaking divorce.

I learned firsthand that what you see externally reflects your internal state. You don't have to master healing arts to understand this. You only need to be aware of this concept.

WORKING WITH SHAPES

There are seven main shapes that I have found helpful for supporting the first chakra in everyday life:

Circle

BENEFITS: Boundaries to help you feel safe and
supported and trust your intuition; associated

with the metal element—protection, efficiency, focus, and health

VISUALLY: Picture an egg, where things are created and nurtured; can be placed around any person, place, or thing for a sense of trustworthiness and security

QUALITIES WHEN OVERUSED: Too guarded, not trusting

Cross

BENEFITS: Nourishment; represents archetypal man and relationships; faith and trust

VISUALLY: X marks the spot; trust that you are being intuitively guided to your personal treasures

QUALITIES WHEN OVERUSED: Blame, victimhood

Rectangle

BENEFITS: Physicality, security, and stability; when you aren't feeling safe and secure, use rectangles to activate more solidity and safety; associated with the wood element—growth, expansion, vitality, and motion

VISUALLY: Picture a door to walk through

QUALITIES WHEN OVERUSED: Anger, resistance, stuckness

Spiral

BENEFITS: Letting go and releasing; symbolizes growth; activates any key component of the first chakra; expanded intuition, trust, or the feeling of safety; associated with the water element—abundance, prosperity, and flow

VISUALLY: A pathway to the Divine; the journey from the outer ego into your intuitive inner soul

QUALITY WHEN OVERUSED: Being ungrounded

Square

BENEFITS: Represents the physical body and earthly awareness; promotes stability, physicality, and security; associated with the earth element—being securely on the earth, grounded, and feeling safe

VISUALLY: A foundation block of safety

QUALITIES WHEN OVERUSED: Victimhood and discord in the four B's—blood, bones, boredom, bowels

Triangle

BENEFITS: Traditional symbol for the first chakra is an upside-down triangle, an alchemical symbol for earth, acting as a sign for grounding energy; a symbol of luck; can attune the first chakra to prosperity and money manifestation; sparking passion and action toward who you were born to be; associated with the fire element—intense creative energy, passion, brilliance, and fame

VISUALLY: A pyramid, one of the most robust foundations and shapes in existence

QUALITIES WHEN OVERUSED: Inflammation, burnout, overwork

Wavy Shapes

BENEFITS: Prosperity and money energy; associated with the water element—abundance, wealth, movement, cleansing, and purification

VISUALLY: Ocean waves that will always ebb and flow

QUALITIES WHEN OVERUSED: Being overly emotional and not grounded in true self

Following are two practices designed to use shapes to support your first chakra. These will get you started, but you can work with shapes in any way that feels good to you. Play with the symbolism and try different combinations to see how they work for you.

ATTUNE TO GROUNDING ENERGY

You can do this practice during a ritual, meditation, breathwork, or just before putting on your shoes for the day. With your ring finger (the finger associated with the first chakra), outline a square on the bottoms of your feet to attune to securing the benefit of the shape. While tracing the shape, feel, sense, know, and visualize the outcome of what you want in your mind's eye. Simultaneously say a present-tense affirmation to help actualize the intention, such as:

> *I am secure in my being and confident in my*
> *knowing, and it is easy for me to trust.*

Explore different shapes and intentions, changing the affirmation above to fit the qualities of the shape and your desire.

ACTIVATE PROSPERITY AND ABUNDANCE

You can use this shape to activate prosperity. There are many ways to do this, from a simple action like placing a triangle in the memo of a written check to keeping coins in a triangular dish and saying *thank you* every time you drop one in. Or keep a written list of all money that comes into your life and draw a triangle on the page or place your hands in a triangular shape over the data and affirm aloud:

> *I am prosperity. Money and resources*
> *easily find me and bless me.*

WORKING WITH COLOR

You can also activate and attune your first chakra using color. While the first chakra is traditionally associated with the colors red and black, you can play with the full color spectrum and consider how other colors interact with the first chakra.

Let's take a look at the subtle energies contained in twelve colors I find useful in supporting the first chakra. As you read about each color, pay attention to its benefits and reflect on how you might be able to incorporate its remedial properties.

Red

BENEFITS: Heals wounds, aligns the spinal cord, grounds energy, activates courage, empowers intuition, kills viruses and microbes, activates money flow and passion, promotes physical safety

QUALITIES WHEN OVERUSED: Inflames autoimmune ailments (best not to use if these conditions are present), state of emergency, inflammation at the genital or groin area

AFFIRMATION: *I see prosperity spread with this empowering red.*

Pink

BENEFITS: Creates safe space to love, grounds earthly manifestations, red (spiritual) + white (power) = strong spiritual and intuitive power

QUALITIES WHEN OVERUSED: Lack of self-confidence and trust in self

AFFIRMATION: *This color pink actualizes what I think.*

Orange

BENEFITS: Stimulates confidence, joy, and self-assurance; empowers; supports feeling confident to trust when feelings of safety are linked to emotions; red (spiritual trust) + yellow (joy and esteem) = helps ground into living intuitively in a fun way

QUALITIES WHEN OVERUSED: Emotions cause a sense of vulnerability and untrustworthiness

AFFIRMATION: *Orange brings the confidence to trust myself and live intuitively.*

Yellow

BENEFITS: Promotes structure, encourages self-esteem, attunes to trust and embodying your personal power

QUALITIES WHEN OVERUSED: Mistrust and fear, anger

AFFIRMATION: *Yellow gifts me self-esteem to follow and trust my dream.*

Green

BENEFITS: Calms energy; healing and self-care; helps heal physical aspects connected to the first chakra (discord at the genitals, tailbone, adrenals, pelvis, anus, large intestine, prostate, feet, legs, bowel movements, the last three vertebrae)

QUALITIES WHEN OVERUSED: Too much caution

AFFIRMATION: *Through green it's revealed; all discord is healed.*

Blue

BENEFITS: Encourages a sense of safety when communicating truth, helps you share the truth of who you came to earth to be

QUALITIES WHEN OVERUSED: Overstimulation, oversharing, unfriendliness

AFFIRMATION: *I safely share my message true with this color blue.*

Purple

BENEFITS: Blue (communication and sharing) + red (power and grounding) = self-trust for what you are intuiting and communicating

QUALITIES WHEN OVERUSED: Impracticality, arrogance

AFFIRMATION: *This purple attunes my intuition and trust to follow my mission.*

White

BENEFITS: The recognition of potential lies in the first chakra, and white activates divine purpose; helps attune to the most authentic version of self

QUALITIES WHEN OVERUSED: Isolation

AFFIRMATION: *This soul color white connects me to my divine light.*

Brown

BENEFITS: Nurtures your place on earth; comforting, stable color promoting safety, warmth, and coziness; grounds you to nature; blesses you with a sense of "coming home"

QUALITIES WHEN OVERUSED: Feeling dull, heavy

AFFIRMATION: *This earth color brown attunes me to nature's ground.*

Black

BENEFITS: While black is a color I scan for to identify discord in a client's energy field, it also helps absorb what is not working; relieves mistrust (specifically associated with physical earthly existence); black healing stones (onyx, obsidian, and hematite) shield negative energy

QUALITIES WHEN OVERUSED: Concealing; too much shadow

AFFIRMATION: *All discord is absorbed by black; I feel trust, and security is back.*

Silver

BENEFITS: Protects and deflects; expands and activates a stronger sense of safety; robust intuition; growing trust; supportive for physical elimination

QUALITIES WHEN OVERUSED: Reflects negativity into the collective unintentionally; indecision

AFFIRMATION: *I embrace this silver shine to amplify the truth of what's mine.*

Gold

BENEFITS: Harmonizes your self-identity; helps attune to substantial prosperity and abundance energy

QUALITIES WHEN OVERUSED: Distrust; selfishness

AFFIRMATION: *Remove and clear the old and amplify with gold.*

Color is a fun, playful way to work with energy. You can use it alone or combined with shapes! Here are two practices for using color to activate and attune your first chakra:

PRACTICE

GROUND WITH RED AND BROWN

An easy way to use red to attune with the grounding energy of the first chakra is to wear red outfits and accessories. It's a vibrant and passionate color. When I feel the need to ground, I have a ritual: in my favorite red leggings, I clean and sweep my brown floors while imagining red light spilling onto them and allow my bare feet to connect to the ground; when I'm done, I put on red socks. I always say and affirm the following:

I see prosperity spread
with this empowering red.

This earth color brown
attunes me to nature's ground.

What ritual can you create for yourself using red and brown?

ACTIVATE PROSPERITY WITH COLOR

From the list above, note a color that connects to a prosperity intention you have. Find a pen, paper, stone, or perhaps a candle of that color. Then write out your money intentions as if they are already here, using present-tense and affirmative words. As you scribe, come into a feeling state in your body as if your desires are actualized. For example, if you are ready to safely share a message and get paid for speaking or writing, use a blue pen and seal it in a red envelope. As you seal the envelope, visualize the success and say silently or aloud:

I see prosperity spread
with this empowering red.

Place the envelope on an altar where you will see it and be reminded of your intention.

INCORPORATING SHAPES AND COLORS INTO DAILY LIFE

You can attune the first chakra in many ways; do what feels good to you. You can visualize, sense, or command any shape or color to infuse the tailbone area. For example, if you want to activate feeling a sense of safety and trust, visualize red there. To feel a sense of security when developing psychic gifts, visualize a purple egg surrounding the area. Or if you're not a natural visualizer, feel or hear the resonance of the shape or color—it works just as well!

You can place shapes and colors on altars around your home as decorative reminders of what you want in life. For example, to activate the root chakra energy of feeling safe when developing my intuition, I place a purple (psychic awareness) spiral (growth) stone on an altar to set an intention to grow my spiritual gifts.

SUMMARY

Take the time to play with shapes and colors. Use your own intuition and have fun with them! If you approach them with optimism and curiosity, you can craft personal healing remedies that are powerful and uniquely yours.

13

RECIPES

Now we come to one of the most amazing—and tasty—approaches in this book: cooking (and eating) for your first chakra.

Nourishment by chakra has been enjoyed all over the world. Every chakra is best boosted and sustained by substances that match its tasks as well as the frequencies it operates on.

This chapter features recipes by two chakra experts. Part 1 provides recipes by long-time health and wellness advocate Anthony J. W. Benson. He has enjoyed a plant-based diet for over thirty-five years, published vegan cookbooks, and loves developing delicious and healthy new recipes. You do not have to be a vegan or vegetarian to enjoy his creations, just a fan of delectable food. Just so you know the differences, veganism is the practice of eating food that isn't derived from animal products, including butter, milk, or eggs. Vegetarianism is similar; it embraces a diet mainly focused on grains, nuts, fruits, and vegetables but can also include dairy and eggs. Even if you eat dairy, seafood, or meat, you'll enjoy these tasty vegan recipes, which are replete with healthy ingredients sure to boost your earth-star chakra.

Part 2 treats you to recipes from well-known chef Susan Weis-Bohlen that are Ayurvedic in nature. This ancient Indian system of cuisine approaches eating from the perspective of balance. Susan will give you a brief explanation of this health science and share recipes that can be supplemented with seafood, meat, or other types of protein. Ayurvedic recipes often include foods like dairy.

Happy cooking!

PART 1

ANTHONY J. W. BENSON

Perhaps you've heard the phrase "Everything is energy." So what about the food we eat? Food is the mainstay source of the nutrients that give us needed energy. It is the fuel that keeps us alive. The better the fuel, the better our performance.

I didn't always think about food as a healing, nurturing component in my life. Sustenance was never a mind-body connection for me growing up and into early adulthood. I ate because I was hungry or my mom made me or that candy bar tasted so-o-o-o good. I never gave a second thought to what my food choices were doing to my body, let alone how they interacted with my energy centers. (Chakras? What the heck are they?)

I was raised on an all-American diet consisting of large amounts of processed food. My worldview of food was limited—standard high-fat and sugary breakfast fare, variations on meat and potatoes, and plenty of fast food. I filled my body with burgers, hot dogs, sodas, Pop-Tarts…well, you get the idea. As a result, my weight fluctuated, as did my health. It was not until I was in my twenties, when I suffered hypoglycemic episodes and health challenges, that I took stock of my eating habits and made different choices.

Looking for answers and help, I read John Robbins's seminal work, *Diet for a New America*. It was enlightening, life changing. I learned how our individual and collective eating choices impact not only our bodies but the world at large.

Convinced this new plant-based path was the one for me, I chose a new journey of health and happiness. I read countless books and gleaned all I could from them. Finally, I came to a personal moment of clarity: what and how I ate had an enormous impact on my mind and body as well as tremendous global impacts.

When I made significant changes in my eating habits and married them with my newfound beliefs, I lost weight, eradicated my food comas, and increased my energy and overall feeling of well-being. I was becoming *healthy*.

I became completely plant-based in 1985 and have been so to this day. Since then, and as a vegan, I have become educated about different foods and expanded my diet extensively. Many people then, and surprisingly even now, wondered what I can find to eat. They think my food choices must be so limited. On the contrary: my options broadened multifold; hello, amaranth, quinoa, jicama, seitan, jackfruit, goji berries, and more! My exposure to newer vegetables, grains, and fruits pleased my eye and my belly and was ultimately healing—and it fed my lifelong passion for cooking, developing flavors, and creating tasty and healthy recipes.

So how does this connect with chakras? Chakras are the energetic vibrational core of our bodies. Doesn't it make sense to be thoughtful and make conscious choices about how our food affects them and, ultimately, us as a whole? It's essential to remember chakras are swirling, concentrated energy points within us; when they're healthy, vital life energy flows through them unrestricted.

In this book we're concentrating on the first chakra, at the root of our body. This is where our sense of security lies. It is all about stability, trust, survival, balance, and safety.

When the root chakra is balanced, we feel grounded, strong, and secure. We ultimately have a feeling of emotional security. Conversely, if this chakra is blocked, we may feel emotionally charged or out of sorts or lack vital energy.

A healthy root chakra vibrates at the color red. Therefore, red foods such as strawberries, apples, tomatoes, pomegranates, beets, red peppers, and cherries provide the vibration needed to help balance this chakra. Healthy and nurturing first chakra vegetables include carrots, turnips, garlic, parsnips, onions, rutabaga, sweet potatoes, ginger, and turmeric.

I want to live a long and healthy life, as I am sure you do. I am committed to being consciously aware, so I eat as though my life depends on it—because it does. For me, being mindful about food isn't about being cool or trendy. It's about listening to my body. So I choose to eat and live healthily, and I continue to reap the positive benefits.

RECIPES

To help diversify your home menu options, energize your root chakra, and keep you feeling safe and grounded, here are three of my delicious first chakra recipes: one each for breakfast, lunch, and dinner.

Very Berry Ruby Red Root Chakra Smoothie

SERVES 1

Energize your root chakra with this nutritious smoothie, complete with grounding beets and red fruits.

> ¼ cup fresh or frozen raspberries
> ¼ cup fresh or frozen strawberries
> ¼ cup fresh or frozen cherries
> ¼ cup fresh beets (skin removed)
> 2 cups coconut water or plant-based milk of choice

Combine all ingredients in a blender and mix until smooth. Add more liquid depending on frozen versus fresh ingredients and your desired thickness.

Raise the Vibration Red Quinoa, Pepper, and Tomato Salad

SERVES ABOUT 6

This recipe is perfect for a light lunch, though packed with complex carbs and protein. It's excellent grounding fuel to get you through the day.

> ¾ cup uncooked red quinoa
> ¼ cup pine nuts
> 3 Roma tomatoes, seeded and finely diced
> ½ small red pepper, diced

¼ small red onion, diced

¼ cup chopped fresh parsley

2 tablespoons olive oil

1 tablespoon lemon juice

Salt and pepper to taste

Boil 1½ cups lightly salted water. Rinse the quinoa to remove dirt or debris. Add it to the boiling water, cover, and reduce heat to medium-low. Simmer for approximately 15 to 20 minutes, until all water is absorbed. Remove from the heat and cover to steam for 10 minutes. Rinse under cool water and drain.

While the quinoa is cooking, grab a small pan and spread out the pine nuts. Turn the burner to low and slowly roast the pine nuts for a few minutes, until lightly brown. Be careful not to burn them.

Gently mix the quinoa, pine nuts, tomatoes, red pepper, red onion, and parsley in a large bowl. Add olive oil and lemon juice, and season to taste with salt and pepper.

Chanterelle Mushroom and Mixed Greens Stuffed Potatoes

SERVES 4

The following is a healthy and nutritious recipe that is warm, comforting, and grounding.

4 large potatoes (russet, golden, or any other large potato)

Avocado oil (or another oil of choice)

¼ yellow onion

2 to 3 cloves garlic, finely chopped or minced

½ cup chopped chard

½ cup chopped kale

½ cup chopped spinach

¼ cup finely chopped spring onion greens

1 cup chopped chanterelle mushrooms (or sliced cremini or button mushrooms)

1 cup canned adzuki beans, drained (black and kidney beans work well too)

Bragg's liquid aminos

Salt and pepper

Preheat the oven to 350°F. Poke multiple holes in the potatoes and lightly coat them with the avocado oil (good for high-temperature cooking and heart-healthy). Sprinkle the potatoes with a little coarse salt (I love Celtic sea salt) and place them in the preheated oven. Times may vary based on the size of the potatoes, but roast for approximately 1 hour or until tender.

While your potatoes are baking, sauté the yellow onion and garlic cloves until they are transparent and the garlic is fragrant. Then add the chard, kale, spinach, spring onion greens, and mushrooms. Stir, then cook at low to medium heat until greens are tender and mushrooms are cooked. Add the adzuki beans and sauté for a few more minutes.

Season to taste with liquid aminos and/or salt and pepper. If you'd like some heat, add some chili flakes.

Once the potatoes are fully baked, remove them from the oven. Carefully slice lengthwise down the middle of each, divide the cooked vegetable mixture into quarters, and place each quarter in the middle of a potato. Place the potatoes back in the oven that has been turned off for about 10 to 12 minutes. The residual warmth will aid in developing deeper flavors. Serve while warm.

I hope you enjoy these recipes and find they help you connect with and nourish your first chakra. Feel free to adapt them as your creativity and palate dictate. May these recipes encourage you to explore and discover others that help you tune into your body, your chakras, and your overall health and well-being.

PART 2

SUSAN WEIS-BOHLEN

I learned about chakras when I was forty years old and opening my bookstore, Breathe Books, in Baltimore in 2004. My shop was inspired by the Bodhi Tree bookstore in West Hollywood, California, which had an entire chakra section! I knew I had to create a robust selection of books on chakras too.

I was also on the path of Ayurveda, the 5,000-year-old Indian system of health and healing, and I discovered that the chakras played a role in Ayurvedic methods of diagnosis. By understanding just a bit about this esoteric energy system, I was able to work with the elements—the building blocks of the doshas (mind/body constitution)—by aligning them with the chakras. It was a natural fit; the language of Ayurveda and the original names of the chakras are in Sanskrit. One of my specialties is teaching how to use food to balance the chakras and the doshas.

After offering a thumbnail sketch of the principles of Ayurveda, I'll treat you to three recipes for the first chakra. The first two can be used in nearly any other recipe, Ayurvedic or not. Then I'll present a recipe for brunch or dinner that focuses on tofu but is also great with other vegetarian proteins like lentils or mung beans or a non-vegetarian protein like salmon. Choices, choices, choices—the first chakra loves them!

BACKGROUND ON AYURVEDA

Ayurveda sees a person as a combination of the five elements: space, air, fire, water, and earth. These elements exist outside of us as well as inside There is no better place to begin understanding the elements than with the root chakra. When activated and balanced, our root chakra helps ground us into a deep sense of stability, security, and safety—there's no surprise that this chakra is associated with the earth element. In Sanskrit this is called *kapha dosha*, which is made of earth and water. Kapha is heavy, cold, and stable. On the other hand, the root chakra can be disturbed by too much air, space, and cold wind; this is called *vata dosha*. When negotiating the root chakra, we need to be aware of not getting too stuck or too spacey. We want to be comfortably situated in our chakra, without attachment but with awareness.

To balance your root chakra, you can choose hearty recipes that help deepen your roots or lighter foods and spices to help release any stuck energy. The recipes will leave you feeling safe, secure, and nourished. You'll be able to unfurl like spring greens bursting from the soil, firmly planted and ready to bloom.

FOUNDATIONAL AYURVEDIC RECIPES

These are two potent root chakra recipes I suggest you make to have on hand. They will continually activate and rebalance your root chakra from an Ayurvedic perspective.

Ghee

Ghee is clarified butter, a food that, when prepared with pure cooking practices, offers enhanced qualities.

Ayurveda suggests wearing clean white cotton clothes when preparing ghee. Have pure thoughts and intentions as well; stay focused and present during the entire process. You might even choose to sing a soothing mantra to accompany the ghee-making process, such as *Om shanti, shanti, shanti* or the tone of the root chakra, *Lam* (pronounced "lum").

You'll need 1 pound organic unsalted butter (or more if you use ghee often). Place the butter in a medium-sized heavy saucepan. Bring to a boil over medium-high heat. Slightly lower the heat and watch as water separates from the milk solids. The water will vaporize and boil off, and the solids will foam and then settle. The ghee will make loud popping sounds as butter is transformed into a golden elixir.

As the ghee cooks, stay grounded and rooted, and·use all your senses. The smell will be rich and aromatic, the sounds will change from sputtering to a soft simmer, and the color will go from yellow with white foam to a deep gold with dark solids settling at the bottom of the pot.

When it becomes quiet and the bubbling is minimal, turn off the heat and transfer the ghee to a Pyrex bowl or measuring cup to remove it from the super-hot pot. (Never pour hot ghee into a glass jar—it will crack.) Let it cool for a few minutes. Then carefully pour the ghee through a fine-mesh sieve or cheesecloth into a glass jar with a tight-fitting lid or a pot made of stainless steel, copper, or brass.

Ghee will keep for months on the counter. It will harden below 76°F and stay soft above 76°F. Do not refrigerate, as ghee can develop mold if it is damp. Do not put a wet utensil in the ghee jar for the same reason; keep it dry!

You can use ghee for all your high-heat frying or sautéing needs or use it in place of butter, adding it to rice, toast, baked potatoes, and more. Adding a few extra dollops of ghee in soup or porridge does wonders to help balance a root chakra that is feeling ungrounded and unstable.

Root Chakra Spice Mix

You can use this spice *churna* (mix) as your go-to for all your savory cooking or take a small jar with you when you eat out to add extra nutrients and digestive powers to your food. This mixture will keep the root chakra balanced by activating the qualities of earth along with the lighter notes of air and space.

> 2 tablespoons ginger powder
> 2 tablespoons fennel seeds
> 1 tablespoon cumin seeds
> 1 tablespoon coriander powder
> 1 tablespoon turmeric powder
> 1 tablespoon dried basil
> 1 teaspoon sea salt
> ½ teaspoon cinnamon

Combine all ingredients in a spice grinder or clean coffee grinder and mix well. Transfer to a glass or stainless steel jar with a tight-fitting lid. Store in a cool, dark place to preserve the essential spice oils and their medicinal qualities. If stored this way, the mix should be good for up to a year.

USING YOUR FOUNDATIONAL RECIPES WITH MEAT PROTEINS

Can you use ghee and your root chakra spice mix if you're an omnivore? Certainly! Many people require some animal protein to boost their physical energy. Go ahead and sauté your selected animal protein in ghee, perhaps seasoning with your Ayurvedic spice. Ghee combined with the spice mix makes a super marinade for baking and grilling, and the spices can always be sprinkled on after cooking. Think creatively and bolster that first chakra!

Meanwhile, treat yourself to a delicious tofu-based meal for brunch or dinner, or substitute salmon as a protein option.

Roasted Roots and Tofu (or Salmon) over Millet

MAKES 2 LARGE BOWLS OR 3 TO 4 SMALLER SERVINGS

    1 block extra firm tofu, about 14 ounces (or salmon filets; see below)

    2 teaspoons olive or avocado oil

    2 teaspoons toasted sesame seed oil

1 tablespoon tamari or soy sauce

1 tablespoon cornstarch

3–4 cups chopped (bite-size) root vegetables
such as beets, carrots, turnips, kohlrabi,
parsnips, and sweet potatoes

¼ cup olive or avocado oil for roasting

1 cup uncooked millet, rinsed

Ghee (optional)

Salt

Root chakra spice mix (optional)

Place two baking sheets in the oven and preheat to 450°F. You will put the tofu (or salmon) on one sheet and the veggies on the other.

TOFU PREP: Drain the tofu, cut into bite-size cubes or strips, wrap them in a clean cotton towel, and place between two heavy cutting boards or cast iron pans for about 20 minutes to remove excess water. Combine the olive or avocado oil, sesame oil, tamari or soy sauce, and cornstarch in a bowl. Add the drained tofu and toss until the tofu is completely covered. Pour onto a hot baking sheet and cook for about 20 minutes or until the cubes look browned and crispy. Set aside.

VEGGIE PREP: Toss your favorite root vegetables with ¼ cup olive or avocado oil and salt to taste.

Stir until the vegetables are coated. Place on a hot baking sheet and roast for about 45 minutes, stirring the veggies about halfway through.

MILLET PREP: Place millet in a medium soup pot. Add 3 cups water, cover, and bring to a boil. Lower heat and simmer until all the water is absorbed, about 20 minutes. Fluff with a fork. Stir in a teaspoon of ghee and pinch of salt if desired.

IF USING SALMON: Squeeze lemon juice over four 4–6 ounce salmon fillets and brush with olive oil, if desired. Bake for 10 to 15 minutes on the hot roasting sheet. Remove and serve over the millet and roasted vegetables.

Once all the ingredients are cooked, place the millet in a bowl, top with veggies, and add the tofu or salmon on top. If you'd like, you can sprinkle on some of your root chakra spice mix.

Notice the earthy colors as you dig in, savoring the textures and flavors of this hearty dish. Sip warm water or tea with your meal to enhance digestibility and absorption of nutrients.

SUMMARY

You've learned delectable and strengthening recipes—and acquired fantastic cooking tips—to support your root chakra. No matter your approach to food, you have several easy recipes to select from if you want to boost that red energy center needed for life energy. Go "very berry" or "roast some roots" or take yet a different approach. Any way you see—or cook—it, you're on your way to increased power.

CONCLUSION

There is a concept shared by shamans around the world. My version of that idea is this:

The blades of grass are made of the same stuff of Creation as the stars in the sky.

The perfect embodiment of this knowledge is your first chakra, called *muladhara* in Hinduism. As an earth-star chakra, this amazing subtle center supports the physical richness of your life while enabling you to reach for the sky. Lucky you—you've been exploring this root energy center throughout the entirety of this book.

Within the pages of part 1, you came to understand the vitality of this hip-based chakra by exploring its energetic capabilities. Intuitively depicted as hues of red, this chakra's light and sound bring in and exude frequencies related to your everyday needs, supporting your desires for a healthy body, career, and relationships. As you learned, the related drive for sexual and meaningful expression is analogous to the love story of Shakti and Shiva. These are the god figures in Hindu tradition that explain how your first chakra energy rises through the spine and leads toward both a functional nervous system and heightened states of enlightenment.

In part 2 you met energy experts who assisted you with exploring the many beautiful facets of your first chakra. You journeyed into your own earth-star space to interact with spirit allies, yoga exercises, body awareness activities, meditations, vibrational remedies, and so much more. Now you have emerged as an expert on your own first chakra. As such, you are prepared for anything life has to offer you, joyfully and powerfully.

May you inhabit the space of your own world and continue shining within the greater world.

ANTHONY J. W. BENSON serves as a creative business strategist, manager, coach, producer, and writer specializing in working with consciously awake authors, speakers, musicians, entrepreneurs, and small and large businesses. He has shared his expertise on numerous podcasts and radio and television shows. Anthony has led a mindful plant-based lifestyle for over 35 years.

WWW. ANTHONYJWBENSON.COM
WWW. INJOICREATIVE.COM

NITIN BHATNAGAR, DO, is an intuitive cardiologist, life architect, metaphysician, energy medicine healer, human behavioral specialist, and international inspirational speaker. He completed his medical school and post-graduate training in internal medicine and cardiology and has authored articles for many outlets. He has also studied alternative healing modalities, including Reiki and color medicine, and is a CrossFit and nutrition coach and endurance athlete.

WWW.WHEELSOFTHEMIND.COM

© Atikin Photographics

JO-ANNE BROWN is an intuitive, energy healer, and author who lives in central Queensland, Australia, with a background including engineering and bioresonance therapy. She helps highly sensitive people find meaning in their profound emotional experiences and release disharmonious patterns. She is featured in the internationally best-selling multi-author book *Intuitive: Speaking Her Truth*.

HTTPS://WWW.JOANNEINTUITIVE.COM

© Michelle Francesconi

AMANDA HUGGINS is an anxiety and mindfulness coach, certified yoga instructor, podcast host, author, and speaker. Her signature "Scientific, Spiritual, Practical" approach has helped thousands achieve transformation in mind, body, and soul. Besides presenting online courses, Amanda offers guidance on her podcast, *Anxiety Talks with Amanda*, and has an online community of over a half million followers.

INSTAGRAM AND TIKTOK @ITSAMANDAHUGGINS
HTTPS://AMANDAHUGGINSCOACHING.COM/